LEADERSHIP IN PLANNING

Being an effective city planner means being an effective leader. You need to be prepared to convince people that good planning matters. Often a well-written, thoughtful and inclusive plan doesn't result in meaningful action, because planners don't show leadership skills. At some point, some city planners become cynical and worn down, wondering why no one listens to them but not doing the self-reflection about how that could change.

Leadership in Planning explains how to get support for planning initiatives so they don't just fade from memory. It will guide city planners to think less about organizational charts and more about:

- being a respected voice within your organization, both with staff and with your boss;
- being a good communicator with people outside your organization; and
- being able to understand how and when to push for good planning ideas to turn them into actions.

Along the way, case studies bring these concepts to the real world of municipal planning. In addition, past planning figures' actions are explored to see what they did right and what mistakes they made.

Jeff Levine, AICP, works to make better communities. After 25 years as a planner in local government in New England, including 15 years as a planning director, he now trains the next generation of planners as a faculty member in the Department of Urban Studies & Planning at the Massachusetts Institute of Technology. He also consults with public agencies and developers on urban planning and development issues.

"Jeff Levine sets the stage with his 'leading is a dance' and shows us the difference between planning leadership, planning management, and strategic planning. He explores what planning leadership means, what success looks like, and the importance of vision, risk taking and advocacy balanced with listing, inclusion, and respect for communities. Jeff's learning the lessons from past planning should be required reading for emerging planners and planning theory classes. His simple graphics help tell his story, and will probably be stolen for various PowerPoint presentations."

Wayne Feiden, FAICP, Director Planning & Sustainability,
City of Northampton, Massachusetts

LEADERSHIP IN PLANNING

How to Communicate Ideas and Effect Positive Change

Jeff Levine

NEW YORK AND LONDON

First published 2021
by Routledge
605 Third Avenue, New York, NY 10158

and by Routledge
2 Park Square, Milton Park, Abingdon, Oxon, OX14 4RN

Routledge is an imprint of the Taylor & Francis Group, an informa business

© 2021 Taylor & Francis

The right of Jeff Levine to be identified as author of this work has been asserted by him in accordance with sections 77 and 78 of the Copyright, Designs and Patents Act 1988.

All rights reserved. No part of this book may be reprinted or reproduced or utilised in any form or by any electronic, mechanical, or other means, now known or hereafter invented, including photocopying and recording, or in any information storage or retrieval system, without permission in writing from the publishers.

Trademark notice: Product or corporate names may be trademarks or registered trademarks, and are used only for identification and explanation without intent to infringe.

Library of Congress Cataloging-in-Publication Data
Names: Levine, Jeff (City planner), author.
Title: Leadership in planning : how to communicate ideas and effect positive change / Jeff Levine.
Description: New York, NY : Routledge, 2021. | Includes bibliographical references and index.
Identifiers: LCCN 2020058070 (print) | LCCN 2020058071 (ebook) | ISBN 9780367233143 (hardback) | ISBN 9780367233228 (paperback) | ISBN 9780429279287 (ebook)
Subjects: LCSH: City planners. | City planning. | Leadership.
Classification: LCC HT166 .L4695 2021 (print) | LCC HT166 (ebook) | DDC 307.1/216092—dc23
LC record available at https://lccn.loc.gov/2020058070
LC ebook record available at https://lccn.loc.gov/2020058071

ISBN: 9780367233143 (hbk)
ISBN: 9780367233228 (pbk)
ISBN: 9780429279287 (ebk)

Typeset in Joanna
by codeMantra

CONTENTS

List of Figures and Tables   vii
About the Author   ix
Acknowledgements   xi

Introduction   1

1. Leading Is Complicated   8
2. Why Do You Want to Lead Anyway?   29
3. Leading Your Office   41
4. Managing Up   60
5. Leading Public Opinion   79
6. Leading by Listening   101
7. Facilitative Leadership   113
8. Strategic Planning and Leadership   126
9. Five Steps to Leadership   140

Conclusion: Combing a Giant Hairball   156

Afterword   164
Index   167

FIGURES AND TABLES

Figures

1.1	Jane Jacobs	9
1.2	Jane Jacobs on flyer	10
1.3	Doonesbury	11
1.4	Robert Moses	12
1.5	Urban renewal in the West End of Boston	18
1.6	Edmund Bacon on a skateboard	23
1.7	Balancing the interests of various groups—and your own—is leadership	26
2.1	Leading and managing staff involve slightly different approaches	31
3.1	Types of difficult employees	47
3.2	Union membership by sector	52
3.3	Managing money, people, and programs are three interrelated leadership challenges	59
4.1	How the planner prioritizes different issues	64
4.2	How the Mayor prioritizes these issues	64
4.3	Where is there synergy and dissonance between the priorities of the planner and the Mayor?	65
4.4	Spring Street before urban renewal	68

5.1	Figuring out what you need to do, what you'd like to do, and what you have time to do	93
5.2	A "parklet" in Portland, ME	99
6.1	The Cleveland Policy Plan	109
7.1	How a simple mediation over the price of an item might work	115
7.2	Excerpt from the City of Somerville's Assembly Square Planning Study (2000)	120
7.3	Saint Aidan's during construction	123
8.1	Mapping out a SWOT analysis	131
9.1	Organization chart	142
9.2	Radiant City	143
9.3	Not even Fairbanks, Alaska, avoided large-scale urban renewal	144
9.4	Thinking through stakeholders with whom you work	147
9.5	A Power-Interest matrix, showing strategies to use based on the quadrant in which the stakeholder is categorized	148
9.6	Using good leadership skills is not the same as doctors selling cigarettes!	153
9.7	Nor is using good social skills to lead the same as pushing for the end of capitalism!	154

Tables

| 5.1 | Ways to influence public opinion by risk level and type of activity | 84 |

ABOUT THE AUTHOR

Jeff Levine, AICP, works to make better communities. After 25 years as a planner in local government in New England, including 15 years as a planning director, he now trains the next generation of planners as a faculty member in the Department of Urban Studies & Planning at the Massachusetts Institute of Technology. He also consults with public agencies and developers on urban planning and development issues.

From 2012 to 2019, he was the Director of Planning & Urban Development for the City of Portland, Maine. In Portland, he led an office of 30, oversaw the development of a new Comprehensive Plan, and developed a set of tools to increase the development of low-income and workforce housing. He worked to maintain a supportive and enjoyable workplace while identifying and changing aspects of their work that impeded good planning results.

Prior to working in Portland, he was the Director of Planning & Community Development for the Town of Brookline, Massachusetts, where he worked on several affordable housing developments, including the redevelopment of the Kennedy family church into a mixed-income housing development with new public open spaces. In this office of 20, he had to balance the high expectations of a highly involved and educated populace with best practices in planning.

He serves on several nonprofit boards, including the Greater Portland Regional Transit District, GrowSmart Maine, and the Northern New England chapter of the American Planning Association.

ACKNOWLEDGEMENTS

When I started speaking on leadership in planning several years ago, I did so because I felt the profession was missing a key opportunity to be effective. I never realized that doing so would lead to a variety of opportunities to help planners think through issues of authority, power, and ethics. That would not have been possible without a number of organizations and people offering their support.

I'd like to thank Kate Schell, who expressed interest in a book on this topic for Routledge. I also want to thank the American Planning Association for inviting me to be a faculty member at the Planning Leadership Institute in 2015 and 2016. In addition, thanks go to Planetizen for asking me to record three online educational units on planning leadership and management as part of Planetizen Courses.

While I have generally been a practicing planner for the past 25 years, I am also grateful to the academic planning programs that have invited me to teach courses to graduate students. Teaching started off as a side-gig to help me process the daily grind of planning practice. The University of Massachusetts at Amherst's Department of Landscape Architecture and Planning gave me my first change to teach almost 20 years ago. A few years later, I taught regional planning and local public finance at the Department Urban and Environmental Policy and Planning at Tufts University. After moving up to Maine, I have taught at the Muskie School of Public Service at the University of Southern Maine for several years. All of this culminated in an amazing opportunity to join the faculty of the Department of Urban Studies and Planning at the Massachusetts Institute of Technology (MIT), where I teach economic development and housing, advise students, and work on research related to planning practice. Every day I am grateful to MIT and the wonderful people I work with and learn from in my current job.

As a long-time practitioner, I am grateful to the places that allowed me to grow and learn professionally. I will always be grateful to the Cape Cod Commission and its former Executive Director, Armando Carbonell, for providing me with my first glimpse into the room where things happen. Thanks are also due to the City of Somerville, Massachusetts, where I got to experience my first management role and watch the turbulent world of local politics. As if working through one mayoral transition wasn't enough, I was able to experience three!

The town of Brookline, Massachusetts, took a chance on a young planner and offered me my first role directing an office. I also learned how to choose my battles and learn where the opportunities for change were, in a complex community that has hung on to the Town Meeting form of government despite having almost 60,000 residents. That work got me ready for the most challenging job of my life, leading the planning and community development efforts of the city of Portland, Maine, through seven years of growth, change, and opportunities.

On a personal level, I want to thank colleagues who have supported me and offered thoughts on my work as I developed this book. Ezra Glenn, my long-time friend and colleague, has always helped me think through complicated issues. Wayne Feiden, who has inspired me with his ability to balance leading a planning office and picking up side-projects, offered the first read-through of this manuscript and helped me confirm that I wasn't heading in the wrong direction. Finally, I am grateful to the planners I have worked with over the years and who have inspired me with their commitment to the profession.

Finally, I want to thank my family, especially my wife Kristin, who have encouraged me as I took the time to develop this book and see it through.

INTRODUCTION

As I worked to complete this book, the threat of COVID-19 grew from something a little strange in a city in China to a worldwide pandemic. Now, as I think through the final touches, I find myself more or less in quarantine, though the term we've all become accustomed to is "social distancing." Not a bad excuse to hole yourself up and complete a project, but other than that, it's hard to say anything positive about how it came to this. With the promise of a vaccine imminent, I am hopeful, and that hopefulness infuses this book.

Throughout this pandemic, though, I keep asking myself "where were the planners?" More specifically, "where were the planning leaders?"

Organizing community thought about issues like this is what we do! This is not a normal zoning debate or a long-range plan, but there is a need to organize across professional lines, and communicate good and accurate information.

The International City/County Management Association knows this! In their material on creating a communication crisis team, the local planning director is highlighted for understanding how to address problems in an interdisciplinary environment. Putting together information across the board, synthesizing it, and explaining it clearly is critical in a public health crisis.

However, I'd go even further than they do. Planners are important parts of the communication team, but we are also the ones who understand enough about different parts of this challenge to help manage it. We are not scientists, but we know how to talk to them about epidemiology and vaccine development. We are not behavioral psychologists, but we know that change is hard and people like to hear that they don't need to adjust their habits. We're not (usually) politicians, but we know how to think like one when making unpopular decisions such as whether to quarantine. And so forth.

Planning for distribution of a vaccine—or several different kinds—will require public health expertise. It also calls out for kind of leadership that experienced planners can provide. At our finest, we are able to handle program logistics and think through the tradeoffs associated with prioritization. We are thoughtful about how to make sure people can safely get to and from vaccine centers. We have a good sense of what real estate is available for temporary needs and whether it will work well.

It may be that things are evolving too quickly for planners to play an active role in vaccine distribution. On the other hand, all indications are that a distribution process is likely to take place over months, not weeks, and may be a part of our lives for longer than most people think. The longer such a system is needed, the more planners need to play a role.

Planners are particularly sensitive to equity issues. As part of a team working on vaccine distribution, we would be best able to determine what locations are most accessible to those without cars, as well as those with mobility issues. We can easily look at demographic data and find locations that will serve economically and racially diverse populations.

In general, we bring a breadth to a topic that not all professions can bring. There are lots of reasons to involve planners in such a major mobilization effort.

Some communities understand how planners lead in these sorts of times. Burlington, Vermont, for example, declared its planners "essential employees" and charged them with planning for response to the crisis, as well as coming up with an economic strategy for the city following the pandemic.

Unfortunately, too few places rely on the planning expertise to help with this kind of situation. Planners are seen as the regulators, or the ones who tell you what your cornice should look like. Perhaps they see us as making sure the new roads are built in the right places. They don't usually look to use us during a public health crisis.

It's easy to blame everyone else for this. I'm here to tell you that it's not entirely their fault. We planners have allowed ourselves to be pigeon-holed. After the failings of urban renewal, we seem to have settled into those roles and are happy to take a back seat to other professions in planning for major change. We have generally yielded power to other public agencies, most notably public works, fire, police, and, of course, the top administrators. We may write memos providing background data for Planning Boards and City Councils, but we sometimes don't even offer a recommendation. We are leadership-shy.

It doesn't have to be that way.

Imagine an alternative with of bold, unabashed planners who don't have the baggage of urban renewal holding us back. This could be called the "no filter" approach. As a planner, say what you think and don't worry about the consequences. The place you work hired a planner to, well, be a planner and say what you think. Think the Council President could use some guidance on best practices? Get up at the Council meeting and educate the Council! Disagree with a downzoning that is addressing a citizen revolt over density? Speak widely and publicly about how their neighborhood is the right place for infill housing!

This may be a good way to fight the good fight, but possibly not a good way to keep your job for long. Even if you're not worried about that, it's not even a good way to lead on these issues. You'll likely be tuned out as being predictable, strident, or "not a team player."

There are better ways to lead on these issues. So how do you balance speaking your mind with being effective (and remaining employed)? Keep reading!

Leading is a dance. You need to know when to choose the moves, when to follow, and when to tag along aside the pack. In the case above, you're always choosing the agenda and driving the debate. You may respond that you are allowing other stakeholders to be strident as well. In your mind you may have a concept that this is a big debate and, at the end, the judges will choose the winners. The judges in the public debate, however, are not judging based on points. They are judging, ultimately, based on the power structure in place. Hopefully, at the base of that is a set of democratic values.

How do you learn how to dance? It's hard, especially if, like me, you have two left feet. Fortunately, planning is a profession about constant learning. Planners are well situated to develop skills for leading if we dive into the complex and murky world of interpersonal relationships.

First, you need to figure out if you really want to lead (see Chapter 2). If you conduct that personal exercise and you decide you don't, that's OK. There is much you can offer this world in terms of planning skills. Channeling those skills behind the right leaders will do a great deal to make this a better world. If you decide you do want to lead, make sure you know what your core issues are and keep them in mind as you move forward on your professional journey. They may need refining and revisiting (see Chapter 8), but you need to start with a baseline.

Next, you need to be a good administrator. Chapter 3 talks about leading an office and making sure those reports go out on time and your deadlines—legal and perceived—are met. You also need to keep the faith of your boss and the political leaders in your community. This skill—"managing up"—is often risky as it can be seen as being strident or, even worse, gunning for your boss' job. However, if done right, you are able to leverage a much larger power structure to accomplish your planning goals. Chapter 4 starts this conversation, though in the end it may warrant a book of its own!

Your accomplishments also need to be communicated and hopefully in a positive light. Chapter 5 provides an overview of working with the media and getting your message out accurately. Again, there are whole books about public relations, but as a leader you'll need at least a bit of a summary on how to get started.

At the same time, part of what makes planning an unusual profession is the role of the public in our leadership. We are a listening profession and it's important to know how to be a good listener without being an empty suit. Listening sometimes means repeating back to make sure you got it right. It also sometimes means disagreeing, or at least offering counterpoints. In Chapter 6, I look at the idea of the planner as advocate, leading for those who cannot influence the process by themselves. Then, in Chapter 7, I look at the "facilitative leadership" model of planning mediation.

You will want to periodically assess what you are doing and how it's going. Chapter 8 provides an overview of the world of strategic planning. Given how hectic planning can be, there are also some ideas in there as to how you might be able to use that tool effectively in a short timeframe and on a limited budget. I also discuss the planning experts who think that strategic planning may not work that well in a public planning context, and what we can learn from them.

Finally, in Chapter 9, I provide a set of quick tips for leading in the planning profession. The five steps given in this chapter incorporate all the other ideas and tools into a strategy for getting positive change implemented.

Aren't You Talking about Management?

It's tempting to say that the skills I am talking about are more related to management than leading. If you manage well, so this argument goes, you are leading an organization.

In a way you are. Keeping things running smoothly in an office—or even a political environment—is important. In some situations, where the people in positions of power are already leading a direction you desire, the best leadership is to sit back and help them.

Most graduate planning programs don't spend much time talking about management. On the other hand, there are lots of great books about managing an office, managing a public office, and even managing a planning office. Management is an important element of being effective at a leadership job and should be taken seriously.

Having said that, there's an important difference between management and leadership. Leadership is about moving good ideas forward to implementation by mobilizing resources and people to get things done. Management is about making sure that programs are run effectively. The difference is similar to the difference between policy and programs. Leading sometimes means changing things to make a better world. Management can mean not changing anything, but ensuring that processes run smoothly.

It's very hard to be a good manager. It's equally hard to be a good leader. While some skills overlap, others do not.

Some skills that overlap are:

- good communication skills;
- ability to work with people;
- patience;
- commitment to quality; and
- being organized.

Some skills managers need that leaders may not find helpful are:

- patience; and
- neutrality.

Some skills leaders need that managers may not find helpful are:

- political acumen;
- willingness to take appropriate risks; and
- advocacy.

Some skill managers need that leaders may not find helpful are:

- attention to detail;
- deference to an existing power structure; and
- willingness to get to a clean resolution at the expense of the right resolution.

Many people go into the planning profession to improve the world. As a result, it's a profession that is more likely than many to produce desired leaders. In fact, planners often come out of school with a strong sense of their ability to lead. This book will help turn that sense of ability into an accurate assessment of their leadership acumen.

How to Read This Book

If you're like many busy planners, you won't have much time to sit down and read this book cover to cover. If you go on vacation, you're much more likely—and well advised—to bring a good escapist novel or history book you've been meaning to get to. I've tried to keep the tone light and include interesting cases and anecdotes, so it will hopefully be more interesting than a lot of the books you might read on planning issues.

So when will you ever be able to complete this book? Granted, it's not very long. On the other hand, your time to read things other than memos and staff reports is limited.

I've structured this book in such a way that you can pick sections to read as you have time and implement them immediately. You can move on to the sections that interest you most and go back to other parts later. While ideally it would be read from start to end—that's why I arranged the chapters as I did—the individual chapters aren't cumulative in a traditional sense. Be a leader and take control of your reading!

If you are reading this book as part of a course, it's best to read it from start to end. Picking out individual chapters will work if your time is limited.

1

LEADING IS COMPLICATED

In the world of planning, it often comes back to Jane Jacobs. This is particularly true in the world of planning education. From public testimony to comprehensive plans, her books and actions are often seen as the gold standard of city planning practice. It's hard to miss her face or the iconic image of her holding up documents, whether on city planning social media feeds or in the halls of planning programs. Want to "planner" a normal image up? Add Jane's face to it!

Jacobs is an interesting icon, given that she didn't think much of the planning profession as a whole. In fact, in *The Death and Life of Great American Cities*, she dismissed the whole field of planning in stating (in parentheses, no less): "(The pseudoscience of planning seems almost neurotic in its determination to imitate empiric failure and ignore empiric success)" (Jacobs 1992 [1961], 183).

Regardless, the love for all things "Jane" seems to permeate planning and a field. It's an interesting statement on the current planning profession that the icon of the field disliked planners, although admittedly, not as much as other activists such as Robert Goodman, a planning school dropout who

Figure 1.1 Jane Jacobs. Credit: Library of Congress, Prints and Photographs Division, LC-USZ62–104052.

called planners "the soft cops." In his book *After the Planners*, Goodman wrote that planners were like the people who got the U.S. into the Vietnam War. He even rejected advocacy planning—a popular concept created in the 1960s suggesting that planners can promote equity—as ineffective.

It's fair to say that Jacobs and many of her intellectual peers felt cities had no need for planners.

It's not hard to understand why. The planning profession had just gone through several decades of wide-scale demolition and social experimentation in the name of "urban renewal." Planning after urban renewal was put in an interesting place. On the one hand, the excesses and arrogance of many urban renewal projects cannot be denied. On the other hand, if the true path is to do nothing and let cities be, what is the point of planning? While some turned to advocacy planning and more public participation as the solution, even that role was dismissed by experienced experts like Goodman.

The message may be "be humble." It may also be "don't repeat the mistakes of the past." These are both good messages for planners to heed. But where is the positive direction in those messages? If we should not repeat past mistakes, what should we do instead? Find a different field

Figure 1.2 Jane Jacobs on flyer. Credit: Author. Original image: Library of Congress, Prints and Photographs Division, LC-USZ62–104052.

of work, as Jacobs and Goodman would suggest? Re-invent planning as a tool of public engagement and outreach? What is the role of the professional planner if the entire idea of civic action causes more problems than it cures?

In Jacob's eyes, the leadership of the planner involves getting out of the way. At a minimum, planning leadership in her eyes means listening to the public (and, some would add, the educated, white, somewhat affluent public) and just doing what they say. That's one way to look at the issue. On the other hand, it assumes that you as a planner have no wisdom to offer to the public. If planning is a profession, you have to have some wisdom to offer, right? If not, why are you in the profession?

An Ideal Arch-enemy?

Of course, Jacobs and her peer thinkers had easy targets in the urban renewal movement. Flush with federal cash and filled with post-World War II American hubris, many planners of the day took on very real problems with untested solutions. Slums are dirty and unsafe? Get rid

Figure 1.3 Doonesbury. Credit: Doonesbury © 1974 G.B. Trudeau. Reprinted with permission of Andrews McMeel Syndication. All rights reserved.

of them and build some of those Corbusier-inspired towers in a field! Trolley systems are run down and don't go where they need to? Replace them with a new system of highways based, ironically, on the German autobahn! Worried about atomic annihilation of US cities? Disperse residents into the countryside where they will be harder to target!

Just as planners present Jacobs as their unlikely hero, they similarly vilify Robert Moses. Moses, the target of much of Jacobs' ire when he tried to run a highway through her neighborhood, is an unsympathetic figure. Born into affluence and starting his career in politics, he quickly found a more powerful role behind the scenes in the New York urban renewal efforts of the mid-twentieth century. Tall, well-dressed, and arrogant, he was almost custom-made to represent the concept of planner arrogance.

Starting off as a good government reformer, Moses worked to rid New York state politics of patronage. After connecting with Governor Al Smith in the 1920s, Moses gained early attention working on state parks on Long Island. When the New Deal started funding parks, roadways, and bridges, he followed the resources and entered the main period of his career, where he worked on the modern New York City transportation and park systems.

Moses was well known for being a shrewd administrator and an effective implementor of projects. In some ways, he was an excellent leader for planning projects. However, the biases of the times, and his own biases, were significant shortcomings. He was said to be racist and

Figure 1.4 Robert Moses. Credit: C.M. Stieglitz, World Telegram staff photographer—Library of Congress. New York World-Telegram & Sun Collection. http://hdl.loc.gov/loc.pnp/cph.3c36079.

classist, and many of his actions suggest that he was. He did not spend much time thinking about transit, believing that the automobile was the transportation mode of the future. Many planning historians go further and suggest that he hated transit and sought to undermine it by promoting automobile use. He was even rumored to try to keep African Americans out of public pools by keeping them cold, in the belief that they preferred warm water.

Another of Moses' strengths was his strategic prowess. He understood politicians well. That may be in part because he was himself a failed political candidate. He generally knew what they liked and didn't like, and figured out ways to keep them happy. He knew the politicians loved ribbon-cuttings, so he would start projects as soon as possible.

Moses also understood that they hated admitting failure. A strategy that combined both of these ideas was to start a project before he had enough funding to complete it. Once it was under way and the grand beginning was announced, he knew that politicians would not want it to fail. He would then return to them and ask for more funds to complete the project, and would usually succeed. Later, he would have access to his own dedicated sources of funding through the various authorities he headed and he wouldn't even have to ask for more money.

Bureaucracy was Moses' friend and ally. He was able to create positions in the various quasi-public agencies around New York and then convince decision makers to float bonds to fund activities. Until the bonds were paid off, the organization had a secure existence because the bond holders wanted their dividend. Long before they were paid off, he would float more bonds and make sure his spot was secure. For most of his career, he was involved with several agencies. At the peak of his powers, he had leadership roles in more than ten.

While it's theoretically appealing to admire Moses' survival skills, his leadership style had some significant weaknesses. He had little tolerance for dissent. He had no regard for the impacts of his decisions on residents, displacing them with little notice and no sympathy. His most famous quote to justify his actions compared what he was doing to surgery that was necessary to save the city:

> You can draw any kind of picture you want on a clean slate and indulge your every whim in the wilderness in laying out a New Delhi, Canberra, or Brasilia, but when you operate in an overbuilt metropolis, you have to hack your way with a meat ax. (Caro 1975, 849)

Moses led in an aggressive, military way that was not unusual in the postwar period. It's not that rare today either. It can be remarkably effective if you are good at it. However, it's not a good long-term approach to planning leadership. Effective planning leaders will factor in other people's views and will be open to evidence-based adjustments to their plans.

Moses began to run into resistance from Jacobs—and public sentiment generally—in the 1960s. He showed himself unwilling to adapt to these changes. As will be seen below, some of his peers were more willing to temper their strong personalities.

This is not a biography of Moses, so we are not going to spend a lot of time going through his life and actions in detail. But suffice it to say that, in his time, this approach was not unpopular. In his 1952 book *Robert Moses: Builder for Democracy*, Cleveland Rogers provided a positive perspective on his achievements to date, while acknowledging that Moses was "intolerant of opposition."

Even the *New York Times Review of Books* was highly positive of Moses at that time. "New York thanks God for Robert Moses as a man of action," wrote William Ogden in his review of *Robert Moses: Builder for Democracy*, even while acknowledging that Moses' leadership style was a bit aggressive. "Yet Mr. Moses—if, as he said, he was 'born to raise hell'—is also a man 'who gets things done.' Sometimes this is by means without a taint of legality but usually he sets his course, draws laws to legalize it, then goes ahead in a process of brute force, evolution, gradualism, or whatever the case requires" (Ogden 1952, BR28). It's hard to imagine these two sentences in the same review today!

By the 1970s, after Moses' fall from power, the perspective was far less kind. Robert Caro's classic biography of Moses, *The Power Broker*, provided very little sympathy for his leadership approach. There was much to criticize, and Caro found plenty to work with in Moses' actions. Other books, like Roberta Gratz's *The Battle for Gotham: New York in the Shadow of Robert Moses and Jane Jacobs*, were even harsher.

While most of this criticism was warranted, it does risk oversimplifying a very complex set of experiences. Moses was not the only member of his generation to suffer from post-World War II hubris. In addition, the urban challenges of the time were significant. It's interesting to think about an alternative universe where the significant federal resources that went into slum clearance and urban renewal was instead invested in renovating the existing building stock and rebuilding American transit systems. In fact, as described below, some of his peers tried at least a little bit of that. However, that was not the dominant paradigm of the 1950s.

Some of what Moses accomplished was more benign than his efforts to drive highways through urban neighborhoods. He built many of the City's parks and public pools (though, as mentioned above, he did so with an institutional racist bent). He built some of New York's best state parks. In the end, he left a complex legacy—although on balance, he did far more to hurt than help New York.

Moses Revisited?

More recently, perhaps as memories fade and things become less raw, there have been books that provide a slightly more positive perspective on Moses' legacy. None of them excuse him for his callousness toward residents, or the methods by which he pushed projects through without changes. However, in the current planning environment, in which it seems impossible to do much of anything without public outcry or even litigation, there seems to be a little sympathy for the idea of just getting things done.

For example, 2007's *Robert Moses and the Modern City: The Transformation of New York* (Ballon and Jackson 2007) is a beautiful collection of photographs of projects completed under Moses' leadership. The essays accompanying it are generally positive about his legacy and integrity:

> If he spent any time at all trying to engage in unseemly or illegal activity, this extraordinarily successful man was a dismal failure at it. Rather, we should acknowledge that Robert Moses was a dedicated public servant in the best sense of the term. (Ballon and Jackson 2007, 70)

While the essay goes on to state that Moses was a bad listener and power-hungry, this is a far cry from the dominant planning school concept. Most planners today are taught that Moses represented all that went wrong with planning in the US.

In 2009's *Wrestling with Moses*, Anthony Flint provided a fresh history of the battles between Jacobs and Moses. He did not take an explicit position on the issue, but he notes that others have looked to revisit the debate:

> In recent years, however, the Moses legacy has been reconsidered … Alex Kreiger, a professor at Harvard's Graduate School of Education, lectured in 2000 that while history has taken a dim view of Moses' tactics, cities everywhere are in need of reliable infrastructure—and with citizens continually blocking cities' efforts, it was difficult to get even the most necessary projects passed. In 2006, the *New York*

> *Times* architecture critic Nicolai Ouroissoff suggested that the planning profession had become obsessed with fine-grained, tree-lined block, at the ends of things that actually make cities function. 'Today, the pendulum of opinion has swung so far in favor of Ms. Jacobs that it has distorted the public's understanding of urban planning…'. (Flint 2009, 189)

The pendulum swing had gone so far that by Thanksgiving 2019, author Marc J. Dunkelman suggested that you can blame your holiday travel woes on those who rejected urban renewal tactics, stating that "the pendulum has swung too far." Dunkleman says that the sad state of Penn Station in New York today, and much of our public infrastructure, was at least in part due to our societal rejection of the grand vision. Efforts to redevelop the station had languished for 30 years, lacking "a Robert Moses to whip the stragglers into line." The new mission was to "prevent public power from trampling the powerless":

> In the decades since [the publication of *The Power Broker*], that gospel has been used to justify a whole choirbook of incantations—efforts to require projects to mitigate even the slightest environmental effects, to preserve landmarked buildings no matter the cost, to democratize land use decisions so that not-in-my-backyard stakeholders can reject even projects of great public benefit, and much more. By many measures, the movement to devolve power has been wildly successful. But more than four decades later, the trade-offs have become more evident. Nowhere is the evidence starker than at Penn Station.
>
> In New York, and in other cities, government power is now spread so thin that places once incapable of stopping bad projects now cannot get good projects off the ground. Today, neighborhoods use newly established checks on government to protect themselves from unwelcome interference, as illustrated recently by the success activists had in thwarting Amazon's plan to site their second headquarters in Queens. For nearly 30 years, Penn Station's redevelopment plans have been perpetually held hostage by a long litany of veto threats that rest on those same progressive reforms. And the hundreds of

thousands of working- and middle-class commuters who funnel through the facility every day have been left to suffer through the paralysis. (Dunkelman 2019)

As it became increasingly hard to do anything, even build a small infill development, there appear to be those who long for the power of the urban renewal era. No doubt most felt that these powers would be used more sensitively than they had in the 1950s.

Indeed, urban renewal projects evolved over time, to the point in the 1970s when one of the final federally funded urban renewal plans in Brookline, Massachusetts, was primarily engaged in rehabilitating old housing, not replacing it.

Moses clearly didn't show a leadership style that current planners should emulate. Dunkelman ends his piece by stating that "New York does not need another Robert Moses." On the other hand, that doesn't mean that there is nothing to learn from him.

Moses was willing to work with politicians to get things done. He showed a clear vision for what he wanted to accomplish. Where he failed was in his unwillingness to listen and adjust his vision to improve outcomes.

Is there an alternative to this dichotomy? Do you have to be on either on Jacobs' side or Moses' side? Some of the other strong planners from the same era provide a little bit of nuance to this argument. Leaders such as Ed Logue (who worked in Boston, New Haven, and New York) and Ed Bacon (who worked in Philadelphia) were still despised by Jane Jacobs. However, a look at their careers shows some nuance in terms of how they tried to lead, particularly as they reached the later stages of their careers. In both cases, while the results were often aggressive, projects had a little more public participation. Logue and Bacon also showed more respect for the existing built form, if not the amount that Jacobs would have liked.

Looking at these alternative examples of twentieth-century planning leadership is instructive. While neither Logue nor Bacon provides a roadmap for planning leadership, their approaches do provide some context and ideas.

Shipping up to Boston: Ed Logue's Slightly Softer Leadership

Edward J. Logue was slightly younger than Moses and didn't really start his career until after World War II. As a result, he had a chance early in his career to see some of the challenges Moses wouldn't face until late in his work experience. This timing may have been why Logue adjusted from a top-down leadership style early in his work to a somewhat more participatory perspective later.

After serving in the War, where legend has it he saw bombed-out European cities from the air and began to think about how to rebuild them better, Logue got his professional start in New Haven, Connecticut. Working for reformist Mayor Dick Lee in the 1950s, he did a lot of the fairly typical things that urban renewal professionals were notorious for.

Figure 1.5 Urban renewal in the West End of Boston. Credit: Boston Housing Authority photographs in Boston Redevelopment Authority photographs collection # 4010.001. File name: WE_0021. Creative Commons 2.0 License, https://creativecommons.org/licenses/by/2.0/legalcode

He worked to place a shopping area on Church Street downtown that would compete with the malls, but in effect damaged the character of downtown while still not attracting suburban wealth.

In 1961, as Moses was beginning to find his leadership style less effective and his power waning, Logue was hired by Boston Mayor John Collins to head the Boston Redevelopment Authority (BRA). The BRA had just completed one of the country's most notorious urban renewal "slum clearances" in Boston's West End, and some had set their sights similarly on the Italian North End of the city.

Whether by chance, strategy or intent, Logue softened much of the BRA's approach. The North End urban renewal effort didn't go forward. Logue's one major clearance project, Government Center, is similarly viewed as a mistake today. However, unlike the West End program, Government Center involved primarily business displacement. Few low-income residents had to relocate as a result of the project. Unlike some other urban renewal efforts, the Government Center program also increased employment in the area.

Late in his life, Logue would explain much of his work in an interview with MIT Professor Langley Keyes:

> It's almost impossible to realize that between the Depression and 1960 there had been exactly two office buildings built in downtown Boston … The City was not a mecca for young people. It was regarded as not having much confidence in itself. (Roper 2016)

Logue's work with the neighborhoods involved more compromise with neighborhoods. This compromise was partially a result of necessity. Neighborhood residents were more resistant to large-scale redevelopment projects than they had been during Moses' heyday. More importantly, their resistance was more effective. So it isn't surprising that Logue would give a little more deference to their desires.

However, according to some planning historians, Logue also had some basic belief in equity that Moses seemed to lack. As explained by Lawrence P. Goldman, President and Chief Executive of the New Jersey Performing Arts Center in Newark, at the time of Logue's death:

> He was Robert Moses and he was the anti-Robert Moses all at once … He could think as big as Moses … and had no less ability to implement.

> 'I'm not inclined to generate plans that don't get built' was one of his favorite assertions. But unlike Moses, he was as committed to social transformation as he was to physical development. Roosevelt Island had the most ambitious socioeconomic mix of any new community anywhere in the world. (Dunlap 2000, 1:35)

Logue himself phrased it this way:

> Planning with a community, I've always done that. I didn't do it because some book told me to, but because it seemed to me that if you're trying to preserve a neighborhood you'd better talk to the people who will always know more about it than you do ... In two places I got in real trouble. Everybody forgets the South End, but I let the South End go ... We had this character, and he made a plan ... and I took him around in a station wagon, and I pointed at, I think it was at the piano factory that now has now been converted into housing, and I asked him, what the hell did you do with that building, and I asked him that three other times, and it became clear that bastard had never been walking the streets ... When I came in here, to do the original thing I did for John Collins, I walked the streets from one end of this town to the other. And I got in trouble in the South End, and I got rid of him and got rid of that plan ... Finally, my number one trouble shooter, Dick Greene, came in, took it over, and broke the South End into 16 communities that people identified with, made plans for each segment ... Now that's a remarkable accomplishment. (Roper 2016)

In later years, after a failed attempt to run for Mayor of Boston, Logue went to New York to work for the New York Urban Development Corporation. There he developed housing, including a number of low-income developments. He also worked on redevelopment efforts in New York's Roosevelt Island, a diverse community where he worked on a project far different from the West End development that greeted him in Boston. His final professional role was close to the community, in the Bronx heading the South Bronx Development Organization in the late 1970s and early 1980s. In the Bronx, Logue developed working-class housing and industrial development at a fine grain that would be difficult to image Moses tolerating.

What do we learn from Logue's leadership style? First, he proved far more adaptable than Moses. He started in the same urban renewal bent, perhaps with a touch more belief in equity. As he worked with neighborhoods in Boston, he learned not to view them as an enemy as much as a stakeholder with which to negotiate. Unlike Jacobs, who would have just wanted to do what the neighborhoods wanted, Logue balanced their interests with the larger planning goals of the City.

In Logue's later years, he was part of a trend for planners to change their focus from wide-scale urban renewal efforts to working on finer-grain, context-sensitive developments in existing neighborhoods. Rather than a broad cut-and-paste of highways and housing towers, Logue's final work was developing single family homes in a struggling part of New York City.

Logue was not a perfect person, but he led in a very different way from Moses or Jacobs. He learned with the profession and, by the end of his career, he was thinking like a modern planner far more than an urban "renewer."

Logue responded to changing professional roles along with changing public expectations. In all of that, he brought at least some sense of social equity and understanding of context to how he got things done. As a result, his leadership style was an interesting blend of Moses' command-and-control, with a touch of collaboration with stakeholders mixed in. Whether that was because he believed in this approach or had to due to the social upheaval of the 1960s is unclear. It's possible that an Ed Logue who was ten years older would have simply followed Moses' model.

Certainly, Jacobs didn't think much of Logue. When asked about him, she responded simply "I thought he was a very destructive man" (Gopnik 2019, 78). But Lisbeth Cohen's recent biography of Logue—surprisingly, the first comprehensive look at his career, almost 25 years after his retirement—was generally sympathetic and felt Logue's natural leadership style brought a sense of equity to the table (Cohen 2019).

Edmund Bacon: A Planner at Heart and as a Leader

While Moses brought his authoritarian style to the Big Apple and while Logue launched his career in New Haven, Edmund Bacon brought a third leadership style to planning Philadelphia. According to Scott Gabriel

Knowles: "In the end, Bacon believed that strong plans were the beginning of compromises and collaborations that could restructure the metropolis as it moved into the space age and beyond" (Knowles 2009, 4).

From a similarly well-off background, Edmund Bacon started his career in Flint, Michigan. Unlike Moses or Logue, Bacon was more of a pure planner, who had to rely on the power of a compelling plan to encourage others to spend money building things. However, he proved to be remarkably effective at that role. In doing so, his approach and experiences show some of the most interesting lessons in terms of how to lead as an urban planner.

Speaking of his early, difficult experiences in Flint, Bacon said "I was thrown out of Flint in disgrace. But I had learned that city planning is a combination of social input as well as design" (Knowles 2009, 26). It seems likely that this early experience provided him with some understanding that leadership takes collaboration.

As Bacon moved into his long-held position with the Philadelphia City Planning Commission, his tone softened somewhat. This may be in part because he was not usually the one *doing* the actual development, but the one *planning* for it. Even the plans, showed a softer touch, compared to other planning efforts in that era. However, his approach still seems firm and uncompromising by today's standards.

When Bacon planned for urban renewal on Society Hill, he saw a role for clearance and for the now-dreaded towers in a park. He sought to demolish some historic buildings to allow for more circulation and open space. However, he also saw the value of preserving some historic buildings as part of a balanced urban design approach. That approach could either irritate everyone or show some mature compromise that is the sign of planning leadership.

Bacon may be the only planner ever to appear on the cover of a major US magazine. Appearing on the cover of *Time* in 1964 must have been a high point for his public image. At the time, the magazine, talking of Bacon's writings about Philadelphia in 2009, wrote:

> Certainly a number of Philadelphia's projects built in the 1950s and 1960s leave much to be desired. Still, planners in 2009 have much to learn from Edmund Bacon—if not from his ideas, then from his methodology. Edmund Bacon's fame and his lasting influence largely stem from his ability to forge the link between planning and implementation, creating a new role for the city planner as both an active civic participant

and salesman of ideas. This was just as rare a feature for planners in 1959 as it is today. The challenge for planners in 2009 is to understand and excel at this subtle art of selling ideas, inspiring decision makers to adopt ideas and transform them into a vivid reality. (Knowles 2009, 51)

This idea of planner not just as the one with the ideas, but as the one who has to sell people on them was a bit of a breakthrough. Bacon understood that people wouldn't follow a planner just because he or she was smart. He knew that part of leading for good planning meant convincing people that your ideas are good. This is even more valid with a disjointed public that doesn't trust government than it was in his time.

Figure 1.6 Edmund Bacon on a skateboard. Credit: Edmund N. Bacon Collection 292, The Architectural Archives, University of Pennsylvania.

Even Bacon's image suffered as the country rejected authority figures in the late 1960s. While once generally respected as well-meaning, by the end of his career, Bacon's approach to grassroots activism and emerging public hostility for any sort of top-down planning took its toll. As Gregory Heller wrote in his essay on Bacon's life:

> Throughout his career, Bacon wrote extensively about the need to plan with the public, developing plans through what he termed 'democratic feedback.' However, by the end of his 21-year tenure, segments of the public and the media viewed Bacon as a stubborn and forceful 'top-down' type of city planner. (Knowles 2009, 21)

On the other hand, when community activists in Philadelphia sought a natural ally to protect skateboarding in the famous "LOVE" park in 2002, Bacon came out of retirement to go to bat for them. The 92-year-old Bacon skated across the park in defiance of a mayoral ban and made the following statement:

> I conceived LOVE Park … I make no claim to be a leader, but by God I am a person and I stand up to Mayor Street and tell him to go to Hell and stay there until he sees the light and changes his ways by going to LOVE Park each day with a smile on his face and a warm welcoming handshake, to greet the skateboarders of the world. (Heller and Garvin 2013, 225)

Sadly, despite Bacon's involvement and the support of most of the public, this effort to restore skateboarding to the park was ultimately unsuccessful. Nonetheless, it shows Bacon's understanding of the value of trying to sell a concept, not just say it. It's hard to imagine Robert Moses, or even Ed Logue, doing this. It's not even clear if Jane Jacobs would have.

Planning Leadership Today

Of course, most of this is ancient history to today's young ambitious planners. Nothing that Moses, Bacon, Jacobs, or Logue did in the twentieth century is necessarily relevant to the challenges facing them. Climate change, paralysis of development by complex zoning tools, and urban agriculture are far more pertinent issues. Subdivisions that were built on farmland while these actors fought in the cities impacted our ability to provide food. Flooding is getting worse every year, likely due to climate change. People graduating from college today can't afford housing. We have real problems!

Marx said that history repeats itself, the first time as tragedy, the second time as farce. There's nothing farcical about the issues facing planning today. In fact, the challenges we face are at least in part due to the dichotomy of past planning concepts. When everyone is either anti-establishment libertarians or heavy-handed government bureaucrats, cities are likely to suffer.

One way in which a similar dichotomy is playing out today is in the NIMBY/YIMBY debate. NIMBY (or "Not in My Backyard") is a familiar acronym for those who traditionally oppose new development or upzoning. The term has been around for a long time and partially comes out of the tradition of those opposed to urban renewal. It also is partially based on environmental concerns. Traffic is often also mentioned as a reason to oppose development. Interestingly, very few people want to be labelled as "NIMBY!"

YIMBY is a much newer idea—"Yes In My Backyard." The idea behind the YIMBY movement is that new infill development is good for cities. Often, affordable housing and equity are reasons people support YIMBY efforts. Interestingly, just as some people are "NIMBY" because they want to protect the environment, many YIMBY advocates also believe that their view will protect the environment. New infill means less land will be used for development and also that people are more likely to be able to walk or take public transit rather than driving alone.

So would Jane Jacobs be a NIMBY today? It's easy to suspect so. That puts today's planners in an interesting position. On the one hand, as far as planning is concerned, Jacobs won the battle of urban renewal in the 1950s and 1960s. She is the one whose face is on planning memes and is studied in graduate programs.

On the other hand, today those same planning schools and memes criticize NIMBY activism as being exclusionary and anti-planning. Good plans are voted down by neighbors who are concerned about the impacts on their homes. Often the opponents cite Jacobs herself in their arguments! Clearly things are a little more complex than they initially seem.

Of course, nothing is simple in planning. What some may label a "NIMBY" attitude is also sometimes based on legitimate planning concerns. Development should minimize impacts on wetlands and other sensitive environmental areas. You don't want more housing in places where the utilities or roads or transit systems can't handle additional development. Some of the original ideas around sound urban planning can also be seen as NIMBY ideas. While many may use the ideas simply because they don't want more people living near them, others have legitimate concerns.

Consider the common phrase that opens a resident's public testimony opposed to a project: "I'm not anti-development but ..." It's often a sign that they are actually anti-development. However, it also may be a sign that the person has thought about planning issues and thinks the right place for development is along a major transit corridor, not in the middle of the town forest.

So how does a planning leader find a way forward on this issue? Is it simply housing and equity versus endangered species and open space? Or is it a three-dimensional game of chess of various complex issues that need to be threaded carefully?

In the last few years, in particular because housing costs are so high in some cities, the YIMBY argument seems to be winning the day. Younger Americans feel that they are shut out of the American Dream because they can't afford to live like their parents did. What used to be significant planning issues are sometimes dismissed as excuses to avoid dealing with this generational issue.

Housing planner and local activist Jesse Benson-Kenanav is a perfect example of the "young planner" who is clearly on the YIMBY side. He's even founded one of the largest YIMBY groups in the Boston area.

Figure 1.7 Balancing the interests of various groups—and your own—is leadership. Credit: Author.

Benson-Kenanav believes in good planning, but says that often residents opposed to new development ignore plans they don't agree with. "They move away from where the planning is going," he says of local residents opposed to new development in Cambridge, Massachusetts, where he served as head of the local YIMBY group A Better Cambridge (Benson-Kenanav 2019).

Sometimes, Benson-Kenanav says, those opposed to development simply ask for another plan. In Cambridge, he says a new city-wide plan called Envision Cambridge started, in part, due to concerns about development initiatives that had come from earlier plans. The idea was that a city-wide plan was needed to put those local plans into context.

The plan, as many do, took a balanced approach to development issues. For this reason, Benson-Kenanav says, it "will probably by shelved" by many. "No one is willing to accept the results of a planning process that they don't like."

This may also apply to those supporting new development. In Portland, Maine, a careful height study was completed to explore what heights make sense downtown. The study recommended that the tallest buildings should be along the spine of the hill, along the main drag on Congress Street. However, as tall buildings are proposed elsewhere in the city, those who support new development dismiss the study and the zoning enacted from it as "Baby Boomer planning" that was designed to keep development away.

What's a Planning Leader to Do?

Your job as a leader in planning is to jump into this fray and find a path forward. As with many public debates, it gets very negative and personal. You may be called names. You also may be ignored if people don't like what you have to say. At the same time, as you will read later, even as a leader you may not be able to control the results. What you can do is be persistent but also cordial.

You may not get everything entirely correct. Ed Logue and Ed Bacon made many mistakes in their careers, and are still vilified by many residents of Boston and Philadelphia. They were products of their time, as is Benson-Kenanav. He is also likely making some mistakes. If you choose to be a leader in planning, you are also likely to make some mistakes. What good leaders do is to take what they learn and apply it in good faith. That's what you should do as well.

Bibliography

Ballon, Hilary and Jackson, Kenneth T. 2007. *Robert Moses and the Modern City: The Transformation of New York.* New York: W.W. Norton.

Benson-Kenanav, Jesse. 2019. Personal interview, December 4.

Caro, Robert. 1975. *The Power Broker: Robert Moses and the Fall of New York.* New York: Vintage Books.

Cohen, Lisbeth. 2019. *Saving America's Cities: Ed Logue and the Struggle to Renew Urban America in the Suburban Age.* New York: Farrar, Straus & Giroux.

Dunkelman, Marc J. 2019. "This is Why Your Holiday Travel Is Awful." *Politico*, November 20. https://www.politico.com/news/magazine/2019/11/29/penn-station-robert-caro-073564.

Dunlap, David. 2000. "Edward Logue, Visionary City Planner, Is Remembered." *New York Times*, April 23.

Flint, Anthony. 2009. *Wrestling with Moses: How Jane Jacobs Took on New York's Master Builder and Transformed the American City.* New York: Random House.

Goodman, Robert. 1973. *After the Planners.* New York: Simon & Schuster.

Gopnik, Adam. 2019. "We Built this City." *New Yorker*, October 28. 78–82.

Gratz, Roberta Brandes. 2010. *The Battle for Gotham: New York in the Shadow of Robert Moses and Jane Jacobs.* New York: Nation Books.

Heller, Gregory and Garvin, Alexander. 2013. *Ed Bacon: Planning, Politics, and the Building of Modern Philadelphia.* Philadelphia: University of Pennsylvania Press.

Jacobs, Jane. 1992 [1961]. *The Death and Life of Great American Cities.* New York: Vintage Books.

Knowles, Scott Gabriel. 2009. *Imagining Philadelphia: Edmund Bacon and the Future of the City.* Philadelphia: University of Pennsylvania Press.

Ogden, William. 1952. "New York's Man of Many Jobs," *New York Times Book Review*, October 19.

Roper, Michael (director). 2016. "City Builder: An Interview with Ed Logue, Administrator of the Boston Redevelopment Authority from 1960–67 / Conducted by Langley Keyes." Cambridge, MA: MIT Libraries, Curation & Preservation Services.

2

WHY DO YOU WANT TO LEAD ANYWAY?

Presumably, if you are still reading this book, you want to be a leader in planning.

Why?

Many planners instinctively want to be in charge and have great ideas on how to change the world. Sometimes they have a good general idea like "I want to improve public transit" or "I want to make livable places." However, they don't dig down to the next level regarding their desire to lead that change. Thinking about what motivates you professionally is hard, especially once you leave school. This chapter will look at ways to establish those motivations and how showing leadership might be important to individual planners.

Leadership versus Management

This is not a book on planning management. There are lots of books on that subject, most of which are very good. While there are sections in here about management, it's not about the management; it's about how being a good manager makes you a better leader.

Before you roll your eyes or, even worse, put this book down and look for a book on planning management, here are some of the similarities and differences.

Planning leaders and managers both:

- need to treat their team with respect and inspire them to be their best;
- need to be effective at working with stakeholders outside their team;
- need to understand how to get along with their boss, even if their boss is difficult; and
- need to keep the big picture in mind while team members are more likely to focus on their individual programs or responsibilities.

Planning managers:

- take a set of operational assignments and do their best to implement them;
- engage in strategic thinking about their organization periodically;
- focus on making their organization the best it can be, based on the criteria provided to them; and
- generally want to be well respected in the community and represent the planning profession well.

Planning leaders:

- think continuously about what their organization does and what it is supposed to do, based on the needs and potential of their community;
- adjust the operational assignments in coordination with their boss and the community in order to make it better serve its constituents;
- occasionally pushes stakeholders and their bosses to think differently about planning and its role in the community; and
- want to be well respected, but also want to use their position to accomplish planning goals, even if their image may be temporarily impacted by doing so.

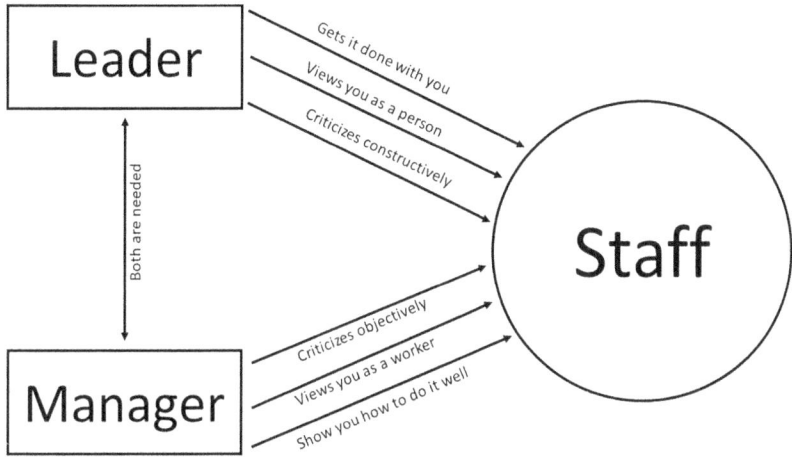

Figure 2.1 Leading and managing staff involve slightly different approaches. Credit: Author.

Imagine, for example, that a major development project comes into your office. It is generally a good project. It also needs a major zoning amendment. At the same time, city leaders support the project and want it to be approved as soon as possible. Meanwhile, some residents have legitimate questions and concerns about the proposal. Other residents have concerns over what the project may mean for the character of their community. Still others are opposed to it because they don't like change.

You have to figure out how to approach this zoning change.

Let's say you work in a community that allows for contract zones or development agreements. Creating a contract zone or development agreement is one approach, and the developer supports this approach. However, you know this developer and know that she is notorious for changing her mind about important details about her developments. It's possible that each of those changes of heart would be another amendment to the contract zone.

You could also bring a change in the city zoning map to the Council. However, there are no zones in the city that allow this particular kind of project. There are also no review standards that deal with some of the aspects of this project that may cause issues in the future.

Finally, you know that your zoning doesn't allow projects like this one. You feel that, based on the city's plans and policies, it should. You also apply your professional planning expertise and know that the zoning is outdated.

You're faced with these three alternatives. How might a manager versus a leader approach this planning decision?

Managers are more likely to go for the simple map change and create a new zone that outlines the general parameters of the project while not challenging the basic tenets of the rest of the city's zoning. You will end up with another zone, but one that works for the project and gives you some flexibility as well.

Leaders are more likely to take on the larger challenge of looking at the city's zoning. You probably don't have the time or resources to fix everything that is wrong with your code. However, you may have an existing zone that covers areas of your city where these sorts of projects should be permitted. A leader would look at one of those zones and propose that it covers the site of this project. At the same time, a leader would take on what doesn't work in that district. If the heights are lower than the city's plans would ideally permit, they should be increased. If the parking requirements are prohibitive, they can be adjusted in return for investments in transit, sidewalks, and bike parking or paths.

This is a harder path. It's also probably the right one for the city—not just for the project in front of you, but for the future growth and development that should occur as well. It's also a path that is likely to irritate the developer, some city leaders, and the public. Everyone may wonder why you have broadened the conversation when they want to focus on the project itself.

In the end, how you approach this project may be as much a matter of how much staff capacity you have and how your local boards feel about different approaches. There's no question, though, that leaders will ask the hard questions and try to solve the big programs. That leaves a better legacy for the community in the long run. It just may not make you any friends in the short term.

Student Idealism

As part of my current work, I review applications for a master's program in planning. I love reading about what brings motivated people into the profession and what they want to accomplish. While some of their ideas may be a little unrealistic, it also reminds me of why I got into the profession. You don't enter planning to make a lot of money, or avoid politics, or avoid conflict. Most people enter planning to make a difference and improve the world.

If only getting a master's degree would guarantee those results! In reality, that's just the start of a long road to becoming effective at the goals most students outline in their purpose statements. First you have to get a job. Then you need to become good at what you do, and build trust among your peers and stakeholders. However, even that isn't useful if you don't find the right time to push the envelope and strategically lead on an initiative.

So, while I love reading these student applications, I also hope they know what they are getting into. These students will probably do great things during their careers. They just may not realize how much work and time will have to go into achieving those goals from their purpose statements!

Fiona Wants to Lead

Fiona went through a lot of potential majors and careers before picking planning. She went to graduate school part time for a couple of years while working at a bank and then finished up full time for her final year. She interned at a regional planning agency and, when she graduated, was offered a full-time position at another one. For a few years she worked on regional planning projects and doing studies for local government planning offices.

She loved what she was doing, but she felt she had more to offer than she was providing. She had ideas about how her organization could integrate its work with other regional services. She liked her boss, but felt that sometimes he just settled for doing things the easy way. Every few years a member community would complain about what they were getting for their dues and he would hurry to find a way to keep them as members. Usually this would involve doing a study for that community rather than work that Fiona felt was more important. She wondered if the organization could offer more value to every community every year if it pooled its resources with other, similar organizations.

Despite her strong feelings about how the organization should change, Fiona had no ability to lead in this direction. Her boss wasn't going anywhere. He respected her work and was personable with her, but it was clear that he wasn't going to give her any real responsibility.

What would you do if you were her?

- You could bide your time and focus on volunteer work and hobbies.
- You could search for another job where you have more responsibility.

Some people will choose the former. It's easier. Fiona was too ambitious for that. She polished her résumé and started looking around.

Moving Out to Move Up

It wasn't easy to work full time and also job hunt. Fiona had to use vacation time for interviews and make sure no one she worked with knew she was looking. Once or twice she had to fly to an interview and make it back in time for a work meeting.

Unfortunately, it was tough to find a new job. She would explain that she wanted to make a difference in the world and had ideas about regional planning. Most interviewers asked her about her technical skills, not her leadership qualities.

Finally, she got a good offer. A small Council of Governments in the next state over offered her a chance to be their Deputy Director. The organization didn't do as much as her current employer and it involved moving from the home she loved. On the other hand, she liked the director, who seemed to be in the twilight of her planning career, offering a change for Fiona to potentially move up. In fact, during the interview, the Director talked about how much she loved to make furniture and how she couldn't wait until she could retire and make furniture full time.

Fiona really liked the idea of being a Deputy Director and had some good ideas about what the Council of Governments could do better. She asked about how much she would get to be involved with big decisions and was assured she would be a key part of a leadership team. However, the current Director emphasized that she was the head of the organization and got to make the final decisions.

What should Fiona do?

- She could ask a lot more questions, at the risk of alienating her potential new boss.
- She could pass and keep looking.
- She could take the position and hope for the best.

She worried a lot about making the "right" decision. It kept her up nights. She even worried that mulling over this decision was negatively affecting her performance at work and even her personal life. Career decisions are hard decisions!

Fiona's Decision

There's no way to know what the right answer is. There are so many unknowns here. What you need to know as you start to explore leading in planning is how complicated these decisions can be.

There are those who regret the paths not followed and those who seem to have no regrets no matter what. Most people are somewhere in between. They calculate risk and make decisions as best they can. Sometimes they make decisions they regret. Hopefully, most of the time, they make decisions they think were correct.

Fiona's situation is actually fairly simple. She is young and it didn't seem that she had a lot of student debt or other reasons why this might become a financial decision. It doesn't seem that she has family obligations tying her to a specific location.

What would you do in this situation? Would it be the right choice?

Fiona: Ten Years Later

Fiona took the job and moved. While her boss at the Council of Governments did retire shortly after she started, Fiona didn't get the job. Instead, the Council decided they wanted to go in another direction. That was devastating for her and she remained as Deputy Director for another year until she got a job as the Planning Director in her hometown.

While it all worked out in the end, it wasn't linear. Fiona got to be a leader, but not in the regional planning field. She loved her new job, though, and found she had a good balance of skills to lead in a complex local environment. She built partnerships with the local Regional Planning Agency and ended up as the head of their Executive Committee. Her detour at the Council of Governments also gave her time to think about why she wanted to become a leader in planning. She realized she had a few motivations:

1. she knew she was good at her job and wanted to leverage her skills;
2. she liked working with political leaders and convincing them as to why planning is so important to the future; and,
3. she didn't like being told what to do.

It took her a while to realize how important it was to understand what motivated her. That was probably her main failing in all of this. The earlier you can figure out why you want to lead, the better leader you will be.

Some people do not want to lead. They enjoy the technical side of their work, or like program management, or simply don't want to spend a lot of time explaining why planning is important to another City Councilor or angry resident. If that's you, it's best to figure that out now and not spend years trying for that top-level leadership position. There's always lots of work for people like this.

Figuring out Why You Want to Lead—and Whether You'd Be Good at It

How do you figure out why you want to be a leader? It's not easy. You're not likely to figure it out while you are in your office. Making the time and space to think about these things competes with lots of other, more enjoyable things.

On the other hand, you're taking the time to read this book. So either you decided this issue is important or someone else decided you should think about it.

There are whole books written about finding your professional direction. You should consider reading one of those if you wish. In the meantime, think about some basic questions:

1. How clear is your vision of what you want to accomplish? The clearer your purpose, the more likely you are to truly want to lead in that direction.

2. How willing are you to have people be upset with you? If you are naturally conflict-averse, leading may not be for you.
3. Are you a good listener? Contrary to what some people think, it's important for leaders to listen to others and be open to changing course when it makes sense to do so.
4. Are you satisfied with the current planning systems? If you are, you may not really want to lead. You may want to manage, but not lead.
5. Are you just motivated by ambition or perhaps by a desire to prove to others in your life that you can get ahead? If you only want to lead in order to be considered successful, you may not have the right reasons to lead. You may want to manage, but not lead.
6. Do you believe you can do a better job than someone else in a leadership role? If not, you may not want to be a planning leader.
7. Do you want to lead because you actually want to be an elected or appointed official? Would you want to be on the Planning Board or a City Councilor? If so, being a leader from within the organizational structure of a community may not satisfy you.
8. How do you feel about risk? Being a leader can be risky. You will stick your neck out at times, and sometimes it will go well. Other times, maybe not. You will need to be comfortable with the likelihood that not everything will go smoothly in your efforts to make change happen.

Structure

Those are some big questions. Getting answers to them will be hard and may be a lifelong effort. How can you be expected to get these answers yourself?

Some people do their introspective thinking best in a more structured context. There are lots of ways to structure thinking through your professional future. No one way is "right" and no one way is "wrong." If a method of determining your professional goals works, don't second-guess it.

One example of a structured way of thinking through your professional goals—particularly designed for planners—was developed by the Community Innovators Lab (CoLab) at the Massachusetts Institute of

Technology (MIT). CoLab is part of MIT's Department of Urban Studies and Planning. The laboratory was created to facilitate the interchange of knowledge and resources between MIT and community organizations. It strives to engage students to be practitioners of this approach to community change and sustainability.

Part of this mission involves helping students think through their professional goals. CoLab has developed a method to develop a "Personal Theory of Practice" (PTOP) that is designed to help answer this highly personal question.

CoLab describes a PTOP as follows:

> What exactly is a PTOP? Our PTOPs are statements, loosely defined, that integrate (a) our personal values that guide our work, (b) reflections on our professional experiences, and (c) our ongoing insights on the field of urban planning from our time at DUSP, all to help guide our future professional practice. They are deeply personal reflections in a written document or in verbal recording. That said, there is no specific format, required content, or end product that constitutes a PTOP and the writing/development process.

The flexibility of the tool is part of its appeal. You can take a week or several months. The key is to work with a group that can meet periodically to support one another and keep the process moving. CoLab recommends having a facilitator who is not necessarily developing a PTOP.

Completing a PTOP can be done with a variety of tools. Group workshops that try to answer provocative questions can help individuals focus. Journaling works for some other people. Having conversations with important people in your life can also help you respond in a way that raises self-awareness. Using cards that ask you to finish the sentence "I seek a practice of…" can also help focus your thinking.

A PTOP is also an iterative document. After completing a draft, you are asked to think through questions such as the following examples:

- Who am I accountable to?
- What are my personal and professional fears?
- Who should I talk to and get feedback from to help develop my theory of practice?

- What are things I do not know but I intend to know?
- What type of complexity do I want to investigate?
- How much is my theory of practice an aspiration of what I would like to do versus documentation and reflection of my current practice?
- How would my theory of practice have been different if I had written it years ago as myself back then?
- How do I see myself interacting with my community?
- Do I want my theory of practice to be a public document? Why or why not?
- What is the vision in my theory of practice I want to start with?

You can then revise the document and periodically think through what it says about your goals as a professional planner.

A PTOP will not, in and of itself, answer if you want to be a leader in planning or pursue a different path. It does not lock you into a future path that you aren't comfortable following. However, this process provides one way to focus your introspection as you think through your professional growth.

Developing a PTOP is not the only way to think through these issues. It may not be the approach that works for you. On the other hand, it is one of the few structured methods for thinking through these professional questions in a planning context. The flexibility built into the PTOP approach is appealing because it allows you to take the tool and adapt it to your interests.

Do I Need to Decide?

Earlier, I said that you needed to determine if you wanted to lead. While I think that this is an important conversation to have, it is not a one-time conversation.

This is a process of exploring your professional goals and interests, and those goals and interests may change over time. You don't enter grad school and check a box that says "I want to lead." Different people approach this issue at different paces and points along their professional journey.

Some planners start off happy to be a cog in the machine. They may feel they have a lot to learn and do not feel ready to lead. Then, over time, they master the basics and understand the current systems. At some point they decide they can do a better job than the existing leaders. Then they work to move in that direction.

Other planners start off very enthusiastic about leading from day one. They are in the profession to make a difference, and the less time they spend in the salt mines, the better. Every step of their professional journey is designed to get to that apex of leadership.

There are also people who change their views a few times over the course of their careers. They may start out wanting to learn the ropes and then become interested in leading. After leading an organization or two for a while, they enter a third phase of their career where they are more content to step back and advise or consult.

Leadership can be very stressful, and people even cycle in and out of it over time. Some of the best leaders take time to do something different. They may lead an organization for ten years, then decide to work for a consultant, or teach, or follow a passion for a different interest for a while. At some point they find they get the bug again, perhaps seeing an organization that calls out for a good leader. So back into the fray they go!

It's important to periodically gauge your own feelings about these things. Are you happy doing what you are doing? Are you still feeling energized? Do you still feel that you are making a difference in planning practice? If you are, you're still in the right place. If not, it's time to think about your next steps. Those steps may be toward more leadership or away from it.

That's really up to you.

3

LEADING YOUR OFFICE

Why did you decide to become a planner?

This question has arisen before. There are lots of answers, often having to do with making the world a better place, saving the planet, creating a more livable city, and so forth.

The answer almost certainly wasn't "to manage a large office, conduct performance reviews, and handle labor complaints." As you advance in your planning career, though, that's a large portion of what you will do. Doing a good job on those types of assignments is important for your professional reputation. It's also important for advancing good planning. Being a good manager is key to leading the way in planning.

If you are in a public office, you have one major different with a private office. Your budget is set once a year, in a hopefully cordial process, and then you are more or less set until the next budget. You are then free to get your work done without having to worry about money, at least in theory. That allows some space for leadership. On the other hand, it also limits your choice for rewarding good employees, as financial bonuses tend to be hard to come by.

Planners as Managers

There was some discussion in Chapter 2 about the similarities and differences between managing and leading. There are definitely key differences between focusing on managing and focusing on leading. However, it's likely that any planning leader will end up having to do some management. It's worth spending a little time on some management concepts so they don't trip you up.

While most planners don't enter the field to become managers, being a good manager is key to doing good planning. Most planning schools don't offer much, if anything, in the field of public management. So how do you train yourself to think like a manager without losing sight of what you want to get done?

There are a few parts to managing:

- managing people;
- managing money;
- managing programs.

Managing people is about your staff—and the people you deal with outside your office too. Managing money is about making sure your bills get paid and ensuring you have sustainable funding to keep the lights on. Managing programs is about making sure you are getting your job done as an office (see Figure 2.1).

Managing People

There are a lot of things said about managing people. Some will say that people need to be allowed to follow their muses. Others will say that people need to be kept on task. Some will say that people are inherently greedy and self-centered. Others will say that most people are good at heart. While these views can't all be true at the same time, they each offer a lesson for how to manage people. As with many things in the real world, the answer lies somewhere in between these extremes.

It's helpful to take some time and think about what drives people's behavior in the workplace. What motivates them? What worries them? Don't try to get to know them when there is a problem. Spend some of your work time talking to staff informally and learning their nuances.

Many of the people you will manage are also planners. Others, while not planners, are in public service because of their interest in making the world a better place. There are also some people who ended up working in your office more or less by chance. They could just as likely be working anywhere. Having said that, they may very well appreciate many things about your work, such as the relative job security, interactions with the public, and location.

Regardless of the details, many people in a planning office are at least somewhat idealistic. How do you motivate idealists? They need inspiration and encouragement. Unfortunately, public offices don't often give you good tools to inspire and encourage. Sometimes you are the one who has to put the brakes on a good planning initiative. Sometimes you have to give discouraging news to your staff. How can you reconcile that with the fact that many of your staff evaluate their performance more on what they get done than on how much they are paid?

Each individual is a little different. Think, for example, of what they judge as a success. A transportation planner may view a new bike lane as a success. A preservation planner may view a saved historic building as a success. On the other hand, an economic development planner may view a new, job-producing development as a success, and that new development may or may not preserve that building or allow for that bike lane.

All of these people work for you! What do you do?

This is not a theoretical question. Everyone is looking to you to make decisions and hoping you will agree with them. They are all presumably intelligent and thoughtful planners who care deeply about their particular issues. If you don't agree with them, there is a real risk they will feel ignored or, even worse, that the overpowering influence of politics overpowered the "right decision."

In short, the stakes are high for you as a leader to do a good job managing.

LEADING BY MEDIATING—EVEN IF SOME ARE UNHAPPY

Fairly early in my management career, I was faced with one of these situations. A developer had an option on an historic house near the downtown area. He proposed tearing it down and replacing it with an eight-unit apartment building. The design was lackluster—what we sometimes called a "cashbox" due to how square it was and how it was designed to maximize floor area over design.

Needless to say, our historic preservation staff was upset with the plan. The building was not designated and probably not quite worthy of that status, but clearly added to the street wall and the built environment in the area. The developer said the building was in terrible shape, a clear teardown. I wasn't sure I agreed with that assessment, but admitted the building needed some work.

However, as a new eight-unit building, under our code, he would have to provide one affordable unit. So our affordable housing manager was happy with the project. She didn't quite understand the concern about the building, figuring that if it were historic, it would be designated.

Meanwhile, the public sentiment in the community was against the development. While some liked the affordable unit, most felt it was not appropriate for the site and that the building was worth saving. Some suggested renovating it into three units. Given what the developer had paid for it, that was unlikely.

In the end, the developer could decide what to do and would likely get approval. There was nothing in our code that suggested the development was not allowed. We would be able to improve the design—in fact, the developer said he was happy to make any reasonable design changes—but it would still be a box.

I asked to meet with the developer. Was there any way to move the building forward on the site and put an addition on the back in order to accommodate the extra units? He was resistant at first, but agreed to take a look. However, he now knew that I wanted a different approach and would find it more consistent with our plans and policies.

He came back after a few days. He could do what I asked, he said. But...

The revised plan would only allow for seven units, not eight. He was willing to do it if he didn't need to provide the affordable unit.

At first that seemed like a non-starter. The code said any new development of six units or more had to provide an affordable unit.

I couldn't just waive that requirement and wasn't sure I would want to even if I could. However, as with many codes, ours was complex. There was an angle.

A few years earlier, in the interests of balancing affordable housing and preservation concerns, the town had passed an amendment to our housing bylaw that said that units within a renovated building did not count toward that six-unit total. The amendment meant that if someone wanted to take a five-unit historic building and add a sixth unit, they would not have to make that sixth unit affordable. On the other hand, if the original building were torn down, all bets were off and they would have to provide the unit. The idea was to tip the scales toward preservation.

In this case, the proposal was to actually move the original building. However, the developer did plan to put two units in the original building shell, and part of a third. Did a building that was moved count as the same building? If so, he would only be adding five units and would not have to provide an affordable unit.

Not surprisingly, our preservation staff was generally happy with the plan. However, they were not as pleased as I had hoped. They did not want the building moved closer to the street.

Also, not surprisingly, our housing manager was very upset at what she saw as a workaround. She felt I was being complicit in the loss of an affordable unit.

I thought about the issue a lot. I consulted with our legal team—and with a little convincing, they agreed that the affordable unit would not be necessary under this scenario. In the end, I agreed that it was more consistent with our plans and policies, and agreed to support it.

What did I get for it in the end? The housing manager felt I didn't listen, at best, and was complicit, at worst. The preservation staff were opposed to moving the building, though they agreed it was better than losing it. The public didn't really understand why I couldn't just stop the project altogether.

In the end, the seven-unit project was built. The house was restored and moved closer to the street. The addition was large and neighbors were upset. However, I am still convinced I made the right decision with the data and input I had.

It's lonely at the top. Especially if you make a controversial decision.

Difficult People

There are a few types of good employees. Unfortunately, there are lots of types of difficult ones. Sometimes someone shares both good and bad qualities; in fact, that is often true. Sometimes someone just has one or more difficult traits.

Many of these traits are universal. However, there are some unusual variants based on the nature of a local government planning office. There are some unusual pressures and challenges in that environment that bring about certain personality traits.

In addition, these offices are often unionized. Unions serve an important role in labor relations and protect workers from unfair treatment. Unfortunately, that role is sometimes misused by employees who are asked to take on projects or work that they are not traditionally used to doing—even if that work is entirely within their job description.

As a manager, you enter a complicated situation when you get involved in labor relations. You don't want to get a reputation as a union buster. However, you can't allow workers to avoid doing their jobs by getting their labor representatives involved. Those union representatives are also in a complicated situation. They are obliged to defend their unionized members. Realistically, they often know that some workers are not truly being deprived of their rights. If you get a reputation as an honest but no-nonsense manager who respects your workers, you may be able to work well with those representatives.

There are lots of difficult people in the world. If you're a manager in a planning office, congratulations! You probably have some of them working for you. Now they are your problem.

In addition to that good news, it may be even better if they are planners. Planners believe in change. Sometimes they believe that things will only change if they make tough decisions. That's all true. However, difficult planners take it to the next level and sometimes feel obligated to make those difficult decisions bluntly. While there is no easy way to say "no" to an applicant, some ways are easier than others.

Let's talk briefly about some basic kinds of difficult employees:

- *The Bean Counter*: this is a common type in planning, particularly in regulatory work. "Did you submit three copies of your application

LEADING YOUR OFFICE   47

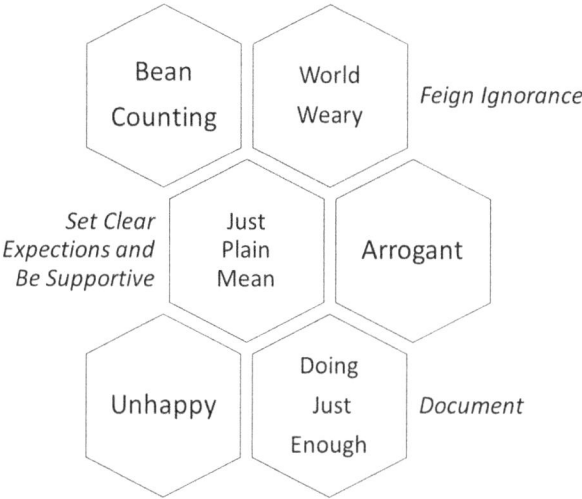

Figure 3.1 Types of difficult employees. Credit: Author.

like it says in the instructions? Are they single-sided? No? Well take everything back until you fix that." The Bean Counter is usually right in principle but lacks perspective. What do you do with a Bean Counter? Help them feel empowered to waive minor issues and also give them some ownership of ways to simplify the process. If the requirement is silly, help them change it to something that makes more sense.

- *The World Weary*: "We've tried that before!" is a common refrain from this type. Usually a long-time employee, they are skeptical that anything can improve and are looking forward to retiring. Sometimes you can ignite some minor excitement into the World Weary with some energy of you own. It's also important to acknowledge that sometimes they are World Weary for a reason. Government agencies are hard to change. In the end, sometimes you just need to feign ignorance about the weariness and help them become part of positive change.
- *Just Plain Mean*: some workers are just not nice people. They like turning people away. They enjoy saying no. Sometimes they will hide behind the protection of a union, but smart union stewards don't want to protect mean people. They can be hard to deal with, but you

- *Arrogant*: this type of employee is a little like the kid who sat in the front row in school and always had their hand up. They know the code better than anyone else and can cite Comprehensive Plan goals by memory. If an applicant gets one term wrong during a presentation, they may interrupt and correct the record. Not necessarily mean, but perhaps with something to prove. You can help a bit by reinforcing their intelligence and knowledge of the issues. You can then redirect them to suggest that sometimes the best approach to being right is to take the high road. Sometimes you may need to remind them that planning takes perspective and getting something wrong in a minor way is not a sign of weakness.
- *Unhappy*: some people are just not happy. I don't mean people who occasionally get upset—I mean really unhappy people. They need support and monitoring to make sure that behavior doesn't turn into something that affects your operations. Most importantly, however, these are the employees that Employee Assistance Programs are made for. If you have such a program in your organization, suggest to this person that they may benefit from reaching out to your Program and seeking some assistance. Actually, that is never a bad step to take with any difficult employee.
- *Doing Just Enough*: these are actually the least difficult of the difficult employees. They do their job, but come closing time, the window is closed and they are done for the day. They may get their work done, and it's fine, but it never excels. They never go the extra mile or like to do anything that's not clearly in their pool of responsibilities. In general, an office can afford one of these. If you can get them inspired to do more, great. If not, make sure you document their work and that they are at least getting the basics done. You may have to argue with them occasionally about what is or is not in their job description if you change things up a little, but there are worse problems.

> ### "YOUR PERMIT IS DENIED" IN THREE-PART HARMONY
>
> Early in my career, I worked in an office that—like many—had an off-site holiday party. There was food (paid for by the employer) and lots of beer and wine (brought by employees). As part of the party, there was a bit of a talent show where staff could get up and show their skills to the rest of the crowd.
>
> One particularly talented musician got up with a partner and played an accordion song. I think it was an accordion, though it's not really relevant to the story. The song was original and was entitled "Your Permit is Denied."
>
> The lyrics went through a variety of reasons why this poor applicant could not have their permit approved. From wetlands to endangered species to traffic impacts, there was clearly no way the agency was going to issue this permit. It was a very funny—and honest—song about how applicants often seek approval for things that they can't do.
>
> Honestly, I had no issue with the song. Most people saw it as satire and knew that the actual process would involve more back-and-forth and probably concessions on both sides. It may have been a little risky to play it during a holiday party that I think may have been recorded.
>
> What was telling was how loud everyone was laughing. We all knew a project that had all these problems. However, we all also knew that a couple of people in the office would be as blunt as that. That bluntness would likely escalate up the chain of authority and be a problem for the managers. Those blunt people, while well-meaning, are difficult people to manage.

Physical Layout

You are a planner, not an architect or an interior designer. Nonetheless, just as design matters in the urban environment, it matters in your workplace. You may have limited power to change your office layout, be it open floor-plan or cubicle farm, but there may be some occasional opportunities to make improvements. Think about how your office works. Is there a front desk where everyone from the public comes in and feels welcome? Are there private spaces for staff to get important work done and make phone calls? Are there informal gathering places for staff to exchange ideas?

Finding the right balance for your office and employees is difficult, and often drops off the planning manager's plate. On the other hand, a planning leader thinks about how the physical form matters. You probably want a front desk for people to start at, with good signage. You may want a computer at the front desk for people to look things up or submit electronic applications, although such common facilities may raise public health concerns in today's environment.

You may want to think about creating a break space if you can, again within the limitations allowable.

Give your staff some ownership of the layout. What do they like about their workspaces? What do they dislike? Is there anything you can do to help, even on the margins?

Different types of staff will have different needs and wants in a workspace as well. Planners may want quiet places where they can think and make phone calls. Front staff may want a way to get a little space from the public at lunch. Social types may love an open floorplan. There's no right or wrong answer. However, as much as you can, make your office layout deliberate rather than what you were handed on Day 1. That's leadership.

Of course, in this pandemic era, all the previous thinking about office layouts is in question. Open floorplans are seen as risks to public health. Break spaces are frowned upon. There's a lot of talk about remote working and the death of the office. Some planning offices are all remote, and others are using a variety of methods to keep workers and the public safe. Not a lot of thought is going into what layout makes planners happy and what promotes good planning.

This is quite likely to change. While there will be some increase in working remotely, planning is inherently a social and interactive profession. There will be modifications to allow for public health and to accommodate employee preferences that came to light during the pandemic, but it is hard to imagine an effective planning organization without some physical presence. After all, we are all about the physical world and how it relates to quality of life.

I would expect there to continue to be large meeting and studio spaces—with excellent ventilation—for planners to meet and work together. They will likely be plugged into good remote working alternatives, so people can easily call in and interact with the other participants. Offices will probably move back into a slightly more private arrangement—goodbye cubicle farm!—with more doors and windows. The common "markup" version of a plan may turn into an electronic document.

This all matters to a planning leader. It's very hard to lead remotely. At the end of the day, we are a social species and we build loyalty through in-person contact. While we don't often have control of our work environment, especially in a public sector environment, we do need to think about how it affects our professional goals.

What's Different (and Not) about a Public Sector Office?

I never used to be able to watch *Parks and Recreation*. I could watch *The Office* all day long, but that wasn't like my work environment. What Leslie Knope dealt with in Pawnee was a little too close to home for me to enjoy in my time off.

So, what's different about a public sector office? The pay is lower (generally), but the hours are more reliable (generally). While there is often talk about "work/life balance" in the public office, that saying may not always hold. As a motivated public employee who cares about leading change, you may find yourself at meetings two or three evenings every week, and maybe even on weekends. You don't have to officially deal with billable hours (more on that later), but you do have to deal with political pressure.

However, you do have "clients." In a private sector office, clients choose to hire you to do work for them, and they may decide they don't want to work with you if they didn't like your performance. In a public agency, you have similar people in your work context. There are those organizations and people who decide on your budget. Those "clients" include federal sources, state agencies, and, most often, the legislative body that allocates general revenue funds to your organization. That funding will depend to a large extent on your success in the past year to fulfill the clients' expectations for your office. Regardless of your statutory responsibilities, this soft factor in your budget-setting process is a critical element.

It could be said that planning leaders must ignore those factors and simply do what they think is right. On the other hand, your effectiveness in the long run depends on your ability to fund an effective operation. If you pursue a work plan that doesn't at least factor in the priorities of your funders, you may find your capacity constrained by a smaller budget next year. So while the link isn't as direct, it is real. I am always surprised by how many planning professionals seem to feel that they can pursue what they wish, without regard to the priorities of funding organizations, and then are surprised when they get their budget cut the next year.

I'm not suggesting that you ignore all your professional instincts and simply make a list of what will make funders happy. If so, the City Council wouldn't really need a planner to provide professional leadership. There is a balancing act between your priorities and those of others. Part of being a successful long-term leader is finding that balance and keeping it over time.

Of course, as a leader you will also have to work with unions. While private sector union membership has declined significantly over the past 40 years, public sector unions are still strong. They are even stronger in local government. So, regardless of your personal feelings about unions, they are part of the equation.

Working with unions is part of the landscape and offers a fair set of rules for management. Remember, not every union is the same and there may be more than one in your office. Unions are there for one

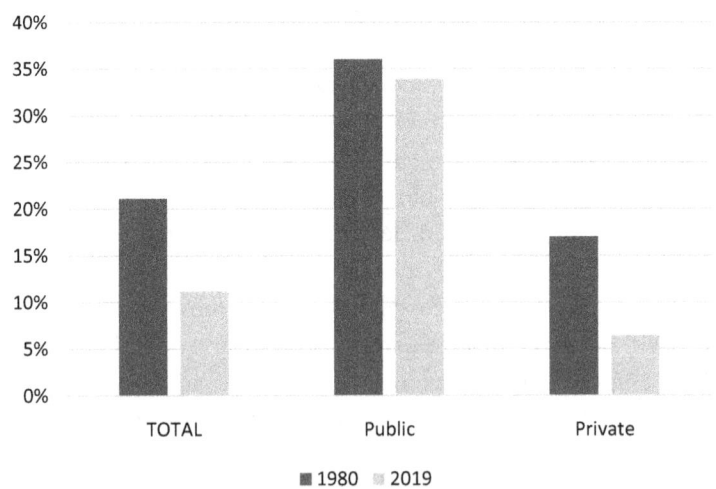

Figure 3.2 Union membership by sector. Source: Bureau of Labor Statistics.

basic purpose—to protect good employees from bad bosses. While they can also protect bad employees from consequences, that is hopefully not their primary goal. In dealing with unions, follow some basic concepts:

- Read the contract. It's the guide to how the game works.
- Follow the procedures needed. Rule followers get things done.
- Not all union members feel the same about the union. Some union members don't want to be in the union. However, that's not really their decision.
- Remember that every decision that is made sets a precedent. If a rule is interpreted one way once, it needs to be consistent. It's very hard, for example, to give one employee flex-time and not another if they are in the same union.

What else is different? You are rarely able to provide financial incentives in a public office. So you have to make people feel valued in other ways. Small gifts help. However, nothing helps as much as ensuring your office is a fun place to work—and a safe place from external threats and negativity. Providing positive reinforcement is also part of the equation.

In the end, however, the first step to succeeding in an organization is to lead a good organization. There are several steps to this—attracting good talent, retaining good talent, and launching good talent off to their next endeavors.

Hiring Well

If you're lucky, you'll get to hire some new staff as part of your leadership journey. Actually, if you're really lucky, you'll already have the staff you want in place from the day you start. That's more of a wish than a reasonable expectation.

So how do you hire well and make your team shine?

First, make sure your first impression is a good one. A job ad sounds boring, but it's the hook to bring in good employees. Make sure it sounds interesting and accurate, and explains why your organization is a good place to work. If your place isn't so great to work in (yet), then explain what you are looking to bring in.

Next, directly recruit good candidates. Make inquiries to people who are solid workers elsewhere. Don't promise you will hire them (you can't, most likely, and don't want to at this stage), but encourage them to apply. If they aren't interested, ask them to spread the word. Good employees hopefully know other good employees.

When you interview candidates, don't let them do all the talking. On the other hand, don't do all the talking yourself. Try to have a good and authentic conversation. Sound excited about what you do and your vision for the organization. Where do you want to lead people? For a good candidate with job choices, this is as much an interview of you and your workplace as it is of them.

Be honest. Don't say the candidate will run a major project if they will actually just manage it. Offer chances to grow and learn within your organization, but don't overpromise.

When trying to decide between candidates, go as much for the good story arc as for the good résumé. Some people have years of planning experience and a degree from a prestigious university, but are not helpful in maintaining a good organization. One of my best hires was a person who had no planning background and got an interview on the basis of a good interview they had for an administrative position. Once they got in my door, however, our conversation and their good ideas about planning and process won me over.

Closely related to this, and to the idea that a good interview is a good conversation, recruit for people skills as much as technical skills. Planning—especially effective planning that moves an agenda forward—requires that element. If you are good at talking to others, great. However, you can't be everywhere all the time. Having other employees who can also spread your message is critical.

Retaining Good Employees (Five Tips)

Once you've hired the right people, you need to keep them. The best employees will have other opportunities and, while you want them to grow and thrive, you also want to keep them on your team. It's hard to lead when you are constantly struggling to keep good employees in your office. Make them want to stay and they can help you get things done.

There are five parts of keeping good employees around:

1. *Recruit Well.* This has been covered above. In addition, remember that your current employees are your best recruiters. Make sure they are feeling positive about your office and spread the word to others.
2. *Train Well.* Offer chances for employees to grow in their positions. If you can convince the budget makers, have a good professional development budget that allows you to send staff to events and conferences so that they can continue to grow while working with you. If not, at least offer them paid time to go to training courses. Within your office, offer opportunities, through "lunch and learn" events or hosting webinars.
3. *Motivate Your Staff.* Show excitement for what you are working on. Also show excitement for work they are doing. Ask questions about their projects and maintain a level of engagement that shows you care about their efforts.
4. *Protect Your Staff.* The buck always stops with the boss. Never blame an employee for something that happened, unless there was a serious lapse in judgment or breaking of a law. Your staff work for you, and when they look bad, it's a reflection on you. Handle any issues you have with performance internally. Don't worry about whether it makes you look bad—leadership means owning your office. Remember that "protecting" is not the same as "sheltering." Staff want to know what is going on, so tell them. Just don't spread rumors or cross any lines of confidentiality.
5. *Support Your Workers.* Beyond training and supporting staff, you can offer less formal support. Ask about their lives outside the office, such as hobbies and family. Just take care not to cross any lines. Offer social activities outside the office periodically.

There are also informal ways to support your office:

- Build teams to work on projects rather than keeping everything formal. Sometimes a talented junior staff member can take the lead on a project rather than the managers.

- Find fun side-projects to work on as time permits. I once worked in an office that worked to design a city flag as a side-project. It never went anywhere, but was a fun thing to work on and staff enjoyed the effort.
- Make time and space for things beyond the usual grind. I always tried to have each staff person working on one side-project if time permitted.
- Be perceptive to feedback as to what is working and what is not. Don't be afraid to stop doing something, like a weekly meeting, if it's not helpful.
- Always encourage employees' dreams—even if they mean they may leave. If a good staff planner has a passion for photography, figure out how to make some of that part of their job as much as possible. If they end up taking a job doing wedding photos, support that decision while explaining that they will be missed.
- Handle incumbent workers tactfully when you arrive. On the other hand, you are the boss.

Handling Conflict

Of course, no matter how hard you work on these efforts, there will be times when you have conflict with an employee. How you handle those situations is a true test of your leadership.

Part of what makes an employee "difficult" is how many different ways there are to be difficult. There is the mid-level manager who thinks they are the boss. There's the staff planner who reads their employment contract and loses perspective of what makes them a valuable employee. There's the "this too shall pass" staff member who has been there a long time and is just waiting for you to move on so that they can go back to doing things the old way. There's the truly incompetent staff person—who may be very nice—who gets you in all sorts of trouble by forgetting to do things or doing them wrong.

There are many more types as well.

You need to be proactive in handling difficult employees, even though it can be very time-consuming. Here are a few steps to take.

1. *Offer a New Path.* Most people can change. The first step is helping a staff member know that there is an issue and that you are there to help fix it. Offer suggestions on how to change and positive feedback about talents that they possess. At the same time, create some metrics for accountability. Then track them and follow up. While this approach will hopefully help, start doing some research about policies and procedures in your office in case things don't get better.
2. *Have a Frank Talk.* These are rarely enjoyable but sometimes help a great deal. Invite the employee into your office. Tell them what the problem is. Sometimes you may need to offer them the chance to have a union representative with them. That's not a big deal. You still need to be honest, within the confines of professional conduct. Explain what you are not satisfied about, why that is clearly part of their job, and have a conversation about how to improve it. They may have some ideas you hadn't thought about, so be open to them. You need to be fairly specific, which can be challenging. Saying "you roll your eyes every time I walk by" is not sufficient. You need to be clear about what that does to their performance and the morale of the office overall. Document every meeting with a memo, or at least an email.
3. *"Hot Stove".* The next step is to enforce your statements about what needs to improve. Every time the employee doesn't meet those standards, there need to be consequences. Those consequences may be escalating and need to follow your personnel policies. However, they need to happen every time. A good analogy is a kid near a hot stove. If he touches the stove, it's hot and burns him. Next time, it will also burn him. That doesn't change just because he keeps touching it. Every time there is bad performance on the same issue, it needs to be addressed.

Through all of this, think about safety and documentation. Make sure that you keep yourself and other staff safe throughout this. Most employees will not be aggressive, even when they are told they need to improve, but some may. In addition, it's critical to document everything you do, so if things deteriorate, you can show that you took multiple steps and were proactive and considerate.

Managing Money

There are entire books on budgeting and on public budgeting, so I am going to focus on how a department head might think about a planning office. Usually there is a formal system for budget preparation and your control is limited. However, there are opportunities to help make your office better through budgeting.

Most public agencies use the previous year's budget as the baseline for the new budget. So the easiest way to find money for something is to propose transferring it from another line. If you really need more funds for something, be honest about what it is and why. It's always helpful if you can think of a way to increase your revenue as an office to offset that new expense.

Develop a workplan for your upcoming year. This will show what you actually want to accomplish rather than just how much money you want to spend.

During the year, monitor your budget. You don't want to run out of money before the end of the year. At the same time, you don't want to leave money in your budget at the end of the year unnecessarily. While some criticize this concept as being a "budget-maximizing bureaucracy," and that is sometimes true, more often you are faced with very limited resources every year. Not using them makes that situation even worse. So if you find your office supplies line with $5,000 extra near the end of the year and you need a new desk for an employee who is working on an old hollow-core door on file cabinets, feel free to get the desk.

A Few Final Thoughts

This chapter has covered a lot, and it didn't talk much about leading. However, managing a good office is an important part of effective leadership.

There are entire books on managing offices. Yet, in the end, nothing replaces common sense and thoughtfulness.

Here are some final thoughts as you lead a complex office:

- Divide the fun work fairly. Make sure everyone has something they are excited about working on whenever possible.

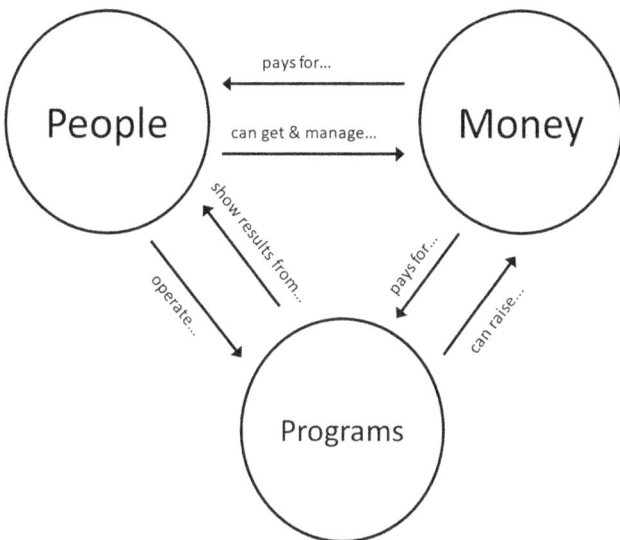

Figure 3.3 Managing money, people, and programs are three interrelated leadership challenges. Credit: Author.

- Build a sense of camaraderie. You don't have to make your office into *The Office* to have enjoyable things to do. What you do will depend a lot on the size and nature of your office. At a minimum, bringing in food once in a while can help tie a diverse office together.
- Think about the bottom line. Your staff need to do their jobs as well as they can. So do you. You all also need to watch the public funds you are given carefully.
- Nurture the next generation of managers. You will eventually leave your office. The people you leave behind and the skills they bring to your job are your legacy. Make sure it shines!

4

MANAGING UP

You have a great idea! Perhaps it's a way to encourage affordable housing development. Maybe it's a financing scheme for transit. Or it could be an idea for protecting wetlands and promoting resilience in your downtown.

You rush up to your boss' office to explain your idea! More likely, it comes up in passing in a staff meeting, or you set an appointment to discuss it. If you're particularly strategic, you bring it up when your boss is in a good mood, perhaps right after she has had a victory with the City Council.

She hates it! You knew she might have some concerns about how it affects municipal finance or the reaction of particularly active residents. What you didn't realize was how much she would hate it, and how unlikely it now is that you will ever be able to implement your great idea.

Part of leading is convincing your superiors to allow you to lead. If they say no to you, your leadership efforts hit a wall. So being a good leader means being the right kind of follower.

In some rare instances, you and your boss may be entirely on the same page. In others, you may have the kind of boss that gives you space and will defer to your big ideas. In that case, first off, you are very lucky. Second, you may be able to skip this chapter for now.

For the rest of us, we have to get our boss to approve our projects. They have their own agenda of things to accomplish and may have to respond to the agendas of city councilors or town meeting members who are not all on the same page.

WHEN THE BOSS IS A PLANNER

Salem, Massachusetts, is one of a fairly small number of cities in the country with a Mayor who was formerly a planner. Mayor Kim Driscoll, elected in 2005, started her career as an intern in the Salem Planning Department. After spending time as a Community Development Director in a nearby community, she went on to get a law degree and then served as the top lawyer for another nearby city. She followed that up with time as a Deputy City Manager and a Salem City Councilor.

Since her rise to Mayor in 2005, Driscoll has promoted best practices in planning as part of her concept of good government. In fact, in her 2020 State of the City address, she quoted earlier Salem Mayor Sam Zoll in noting that "public officials must not be merely critics of the existing city, but be visionaries of a better one."

Working for a Mayor with a strong belief in planning, while potentially a little challenging, should be seen as an ideal scenario for a planning leader. Because in most cases, your boss won't have a lot of background in what you do or why it matters.

Your Boss Is Human

If you work in a municipal planning office or some similar public office, you probably ultimately report to a City Manager, an elected strong Mayor, or some other Chief Executive Officer. That person most likely got to their position differently from you got to yours. If they are an appointed official, they are either well connected politically or, more likely, a professional administrator who has worked in other communities and has a background in public affairs. If they are an elected official, they are probably well connected in the community and may not have a professional administrative background.

Either way, it's fairly likely that your boss is a living, breathing person with hopes and dreams. It's easy to forget that in the day-to-day travails of a busy office. Just as you came into your position with some goals for leading on planning issues, they likely came into their office with some goals for leading the community. Either they brought them to the position based on their values and ideals or they were given them by an appointing authority or electorate, or both. However, it's most likely that they are not just waiting for five o'clock to roll around and mark off another day closer to their pension (That is entirely possible, and a very different challenge—see below.)

What are some likely things that they want to lead on? That's your job to figure out! However, here are some common topics that municipal managers care about:

- keeping the tax rate low or, more realistically, keeping the rate of increase low;
- having a good municipal bond rating;
- attracting new businesses to your community;
- keeping streets, sidewalks, and traffic signals in good repair;
- in cold climates, plowing and sanding streets promptly in the winter;
- providing safe and efficient public buildings;
- giving the schools what they need to function, but not allowing them to dominate municipal finances;
- eliminating what they may see as unnecessary barriers to new development, such as lengthy and complex building permit processes; and
- having their community viewed as a leader in innovation and efficiency (without always a strong sense of what this means!).

Elected officials will be especially sensitive to local issues that may be in addition to or different from these ones. For example, a strong elected Mayor may be concerned about:

- a large development right over the city line in another community;
- bike and pedestrian issues, if there are a lot of advocates for these issues in your community;

- affordable housing;
- labor issues, such as requiring living wages be paid for all municipal projects;
- two or three sensitive local sites, such as a large vacant parcel downtown or the site of a major proposed development in an established neighborhood; and
- whatever comes up at a particular time!

Knowing what motivates your boss is the first step in getting your goals achieved. Ideally, you will find common ground between your goals, either because they entirely overlap or because there is synergy between what you would like to do and what your boss would like to do. For example, you may want to develop affordable housing and they may want to sell that vacant school downtown. By coming up with a plan that accomplishes both goals and doesn't lose the city lots of money, you may be seen as the problem solver by them. At the same time, you are leading on an issue that you care about.

Lining Up Your Vectors

Not many planners started out as physics majors. For those of you who did, this is your moment to shine.

It's helpful to think about all the things you want to accomplish as a planner, and especially the things you want to take the lead on, as arrows coming out of your mind and heading in different directions. The direction in which they point depends on what kind of achievement they are. Sustainability achievements may point up, transportation achievements to the right, and housing achievements to the left. If you are doing good planning, they should all point in more or less the same direction, as is wouldn't make sense to achieve goals that conflict with one another.

Now imagine the Mayor, or the City Council, or whoever you are most accountable to, and their desired achievements. They will probably not be exactly the same as yours. For example, the Mayor may want to be popular, may want to develop affordable housing, and may want to keep taxes low. Each of these desired achievements can be seen as vectors

64   MANAGING UP

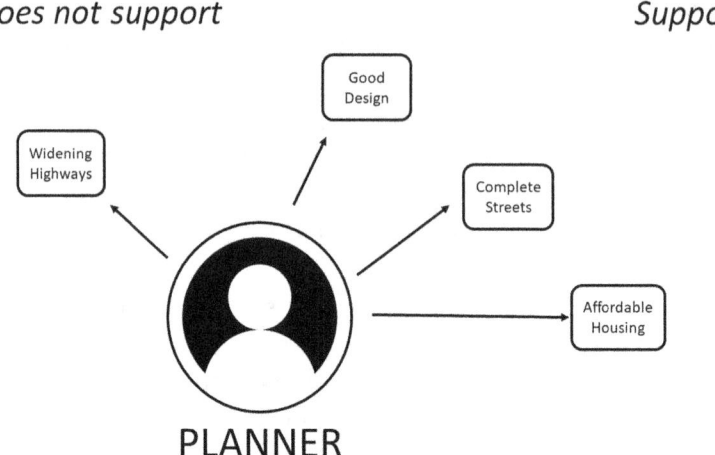

Figure 4.1 How the planner prioritizes different issues. Credit: Author.

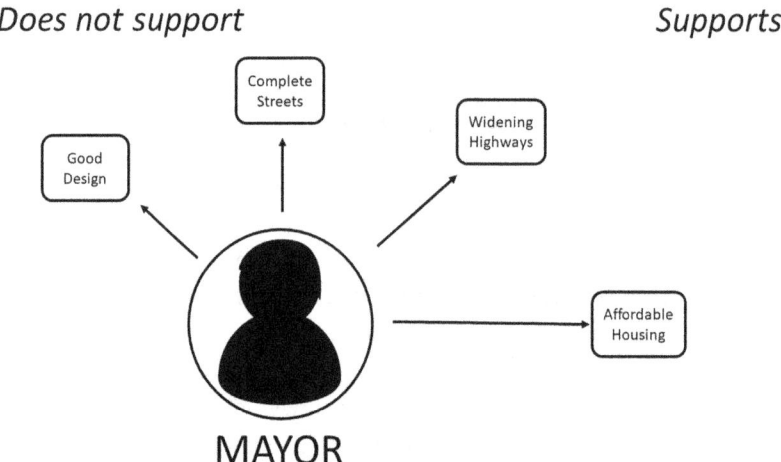

Figure 4.2 How the Mayor prioritizes these issues. Credit: Author.

as well. Again, these vectors hopefully don't conflict with one another. However, they may push in different directions from yours.

Your vectors and the Mayor's vectors point in somewhat different directions. If you try to combine them, the result may be no motion at all, as you push in the same directions in some areas, but in contradictory ways in others.

What can you do about this? Like a rocket with too many engines, you can turn some of these vectors off and—hopefully—convince your boss to turn some of theirs off as well. If you can't convince them to do that, at least minimize the conflicts. You can then start to move in a direction that you both generally support. So if you both care about housing, work on housing. If you can't agree on open space planning, try to avoid working on it.

Sometimes these common vectors are referred to as "policy windows." They will likely change over time, as personalities and priorities change. You can keep hoping to get all of your vectors addressed. However, you should focus on what is achievable given the current situation rather than banging your head against a wall or, even worse, annoying your boss.

This may seem more like following than leading. However, all the best leaders use this technique. Franklin D. Roosevelt had a lot of things he wanted to get done. He knew that each one needed congressional and public support. So, while he worked on social security, he thought about how to get other things done. He likely knew long before the attack on Pearl Harbor that the US would have to enter World War II. However, he knew he wouldn't have broad support or the ability to convince a skeptical Congress and an isolationist public. Instead, he worked

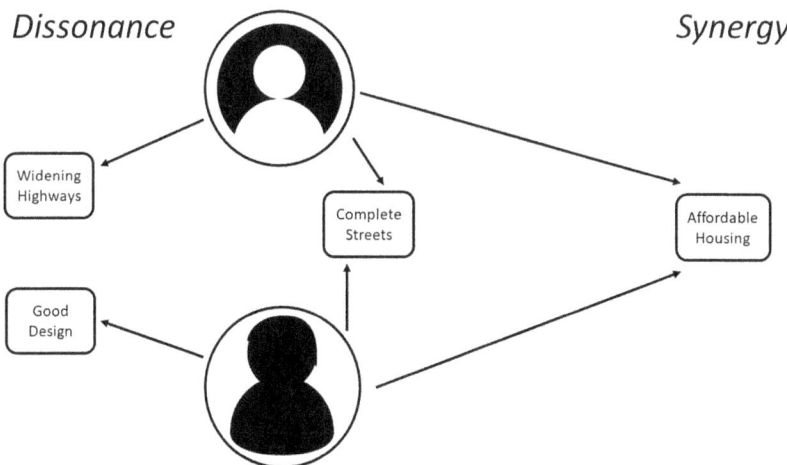

Figure 4.3 Where is there synergy and dissonance between the priorities of the planner and the Mayor? Credit: Author.

to get aid to Britain through the Lend-Lease program, a small vector that enjoyed more support than sending troops.

Doing Management Physics

So how do you know when these vectors push in the same directions? How can you figure out that your efforts align with those of your boss? Just as important, how do you convince them that your efforts align?

This is where relationships are important. You need to not only do the math, but also convince them that you've done the math. You need to use the other side of your brain and build a relationship with your boss. Then, together, you can get some good things done!

Planners aren't always good at people skills. Planning leaders have to be. So if it doesn't come naturally to you, here are some tips for getting along with your boss, while at the same time keeping *your* agenda on *their* agenda:

- *Listen carefully*: get to know what their pet peeves are. At the same time, learn what motivates them. Try to avoid playing into what annoys them. At the same time, go the extra step to help them on things they care about (unless they are things that you strongly disagree with). I've been known to help with a school/city issue that has nothing to do with planning. On the other hand, helping out like that has a lot to do with building relationships.
- *Don't always talk shop*: people usually like to talk about things that are not directly work-related. Sometimes, senior executives get very focused on their work responsibilities. However, they are generally human just like you are! A little small talk about family, sports, or even the weather can help build an informal relationship that pays off professionally. It's also just part of having a cordial work relationship. I had a boss once who had come from the same city as me in a different state. We would talk about the politics of that different place, and it was a fun and safe way to bond.
- *Be reliable*: if you say you will do something, do it. Don't come up with excuses. Even better, if your boss has a problem you know how to fix, offer to fix it. Usually senior managers have a lot on their plate. Saying "I'll take care of it" sounds great to busy people. Again, if you say you'll take care of it, make sure you do! Helping

take care of those nagging little issues not only makes you a good colleague, but also builds trust and reliance in a way that pays off in the long run.
- *Push back sometimes*: if you are having a private conversation and your boss is venting about something, it's fine to let them vent. At the same time, if you don't agree with everything they are saying, it is sometimes OK to say so. Make sure it's truly in private and isn't a particularly sore subject, or one that you know they is not interested in debating. On the other hand, as a planner, it's your job as a leader to stand up for good planning when appropriate. Most bosses respect respectful discussion, even if you don't agree on everything.

When It's Not Working

This all sounds very simple. But as anyone who has tried to make this work knows, it's not always that simple. Sometimes your boss isn't rational. Sometimes you misstep and push an issue that doesn't enjoy broad support. Sometimes a third party—like a politically connected resident—intervenes. What do you do when it's not working out?

First, stop what you are doing! If something isn't working, don't make it worse. Don't continue to push for the city to buy a piece of property for a park when it's clear no one supports your effort. That doesn't mean you are wrong about the technical aspects of the issue—it may be a perfect place for a park. It also doesn't mean a lack of leadership on your part. Bold leadership often requires tactical retreats in support of a good strategy.

Next, assess the damage. As if it were a disaster scene, check out what is wrong and assess how badly it went wrong. Did you offend your boss? Did you make another department head angry? What about other stakeholders, like community activists or political leaders? You may not be able to read everyone's mind, but you should be able to get a sense of what is likely to have been damaged.

After you have a sense of what went wrong, think about how to fix it. Unfortunately, major workplace blowups are hard to repair. You can only do so much. In addition to treading carefully on sore subjects, you should pay special attention to what you can do to be useful to your boss. As I mentioned above, there are things you can do to "make yourself useful" by taking items off their plate, even if they are not directly related to planning.

FAILURE TO MANAGE UP ON SPRING STREET

Nothing helps explain how to manage up as much as an example where it didn't happen. In Portland, Maine, urban renewal had transformed Spring Street from being a typical city street and had turned it into an artery for cars. As part of the thinking of the time, the street needed to be straightened, with a raised median to discourage pedestrians from crossing. Historic buildings came down and the street became a major east-west passage for drivers, while bikers and walkers avoided it. Part of the city's motivation was to attract a major hotel franchise to build a large hotel on the street, which it would only agree to do if the street were made more accessible for drivers.

In 2011, the renowned architect Henry Cobb, who had spent a great deal of time working on projects in the city, spoke before the Portland Society of Architects (PSA) about urban renewal's failures in the city, including the Spring Street Arterial. Subsequently, the PSA held a contest called "Liberate Spring Street" to look at redesigning the street as a more traditional city boulevard. In response, the city agreed to fund a design of the road and work with the state to fund some improvements.

Figure 4.4 Spring Street before urban renewal. Credit: Library of Congress, Geography and Map Division, https://www.loc.gov/resource/g3734pm.g3734pm_g035271896/?sp=27

> Everything in government takes time, but in 2015, the city and the state began making some changes to Spring Street. The raised median was removed. While the original vision was to narrow the street, the high cost of moving the granite curbs made that prohibitive. Instead, the intersections were narrowed with curb extensions, and "back in" parking—which was seen as safer for bicyclists—was added in the extra space.
>
> Some of the curb extensions were quite large and it wasn't a huge surprise when a driver, who was not used to them, drove into one and onto the sidewalk. The local media covered the story, and instead of citing it as a bad driver not paying attention, the focus was on the large curb extensions instead.
>
> Meanwhile, a new City Manager had just started and was appalled by the negative press. He looked at the new curb extensions and—being somewhat favorable to the idea that drivers should get leeway in the city—quickly stated that staff had made a significant error and that changes needed to be made. While staff protested that the new layout had only just been completed, the decision was final. Over $50,000 was spent on significantly reducing the offending curb extension. The "back in" parking, which similarly caused concerns with drivers, was also removed. The city was clearly in "damage control" mode rather than standing by the design that was the result of a public outreach process.
>
> In the end, the Spring Street experience did more than cost the city money. It hurt the reputation of city staff, both externally and with their boss.
>
> "Managing up" might have helped in this situation. Staff could have explained to the manager the new layout and the importance of it. They could have made pre-emptive changes if he demanded them, based on his biases. They also could have emphasized the need to stay the course, well before a single driver drove over the curb and left staff taking the blame.

Finally, time sometimes helps a lot. You may want to spend a few weeks focusing on day-to-day management as a long-term leadership tactic. Make sure your planning processes are running well and you will remind everyone that you are a good manager. After things cool off a bit, you can resume pushing the envelope a bit as a planning leader.

When It's *Really* Not Working

Early in my career I was advised that there is a story arc in every planning job. That arc starts, hopefully, with you as the strong new addition to a team. Unfortunately, you also don't yet know some basic details, like where the bathroom is or what is in the file cabinets. More importantly, you don't know the names of various stakeholders and what assets and baggage they bring to the table.

Over time, your job arc builds to a perfect balance of being relatively new and trusted, but also experienced enough to know who that community activist is. Similarly, you now know your boss well enough to understand what motivates them, what their pet peeves are, and possibly even their favorite authors and sports stars.

This is your apex. Generally it should start when you've been in the job for somewhere between one year and three years. Hopefully it lasts a long time. Once someone giving me early career advice said it rarely lasts past year five on a job. I'm not sure it's that simple. On a personal note, I have generally spent six to eight years at each of my professional stops. However, that's not just a matter of my effectiveness—in fact, at times I have left for other reasons while I was at the peak of my effectiveness in a position.

Meanwhile, as time passes, you start to accumulate adversaries. Community members become irritated with you as you inevitably let them down on one issue or another. Political leaders with long memories recall the time you advanced a planning tool that upset one of their supporters. New department heads arrive and are the new superstars, and perhaps don't agree with you on everything.

On the brighter side, with good people skills and a little luck, you can remain one of the cool kids in the organization. Knowing when to nudge others and when to step down, as described in this chapter, is part of the battle.

However, there is one easy way to turn over this whole apple cart—getting on the wrong side of your boss. Perhaps you say something publicly that undermines their position. Maybe you are seen as working too directly with political leaders, or with community groups, and they are not sure they can trust you. Maybe they're just paranoid and view you as a threat. Most likely it's a combination of these factors. Once you are in that position, you have three choices:

1. *Figure out a way to get back on their good side.* This may involve some complex maneuvering of risky waters. Sometimes you can win a boss back over by heroic measures, sometimes it just takes months of quiet competence and deference. You should think about this option, perhaps test it out, but know that it's hard work, risky, and likely requires that you step back from some of your leadership interests.
2. *Hope for turnover at the top.* Bosses move on. If you want to take the long game approach, you can hope that they get another position. This waiting may take years (see above), but it's certainly possible. If a new boss comes in, there's also a risk that they are not supportive of your work or were told by the previous boss that they think you are trouble.
3. *Move on.* Though it's not exactly what Falstaff said in Shakespeare's *Henry IV, Part 1*, he is often quoted as saying that "discretion is the better part of valour." (The actual quote, taken after he apparently is dead but is actually alive in Act 5 Scene 4, is "The better part of valor is discretion, in the which better part I have saved my life." Scholars have been arguing that it has been misquoted and misinterpreted ever since!) There are times when you are not going to be able to accomplish what you want to with the current relationship with your boss. In a worst-case scenario, you may be asked to leave. More likely, your efforts to lead on planning issues will be continually stymied. At this point, you can step down and decide to stick to your proverbial knitting. Or you can find a new challenge and opportunity. This may not happen overnight, but you can start the process.

These are complicated situations, and this book is not going to be able to help you solve internal issues and challenges by itself. It's always good to discreetly seek advice, both professionally and informally, as to how to mend these relationships when possible.

Managing Up—Squared!

Of course, the buck doesn't always stop at your boss. As shown in any organizational chart, bosses often have bosses. In government, the ultimate bosses are the residents of the community, whether directly or through an elected legislative body. So, getting your boss on board with your big ideas may not be the only step toward getting them achieved. On the other hand, having support from above your pay grade can't hurt either.

Assuming you have your boss' support, how do you take it to the next step and make sure that this support runs up the food chain? Deliberatively. You will need to tap into their support and plan an approach to getting decision makers' support. This will involve some of the strategic planning tools that will be discussed later, and it will also involve a delicate dance of lining up as much goodwill and trust as you can.

Part of how to help your boss help you depends on how emphatic their support for your ideas is. While it's sometimes hard to tell for sure, it's important to get a sense of whether they are generally supportive or truly willing to fight for the same ideas.

I once had a boss who was great at supporting me in person. Almost any time I came to him with an idea, he would signal his support for it. I would go back to my office confident that I had the City Manager's support in implementing my plans. With that confidence, I'd host meetings of staff from various departments and assign tasks to planners. We were going to get this idea done!

Sometimes I would sense that he was a little wary of some aspect of my plans. I would adjust accordingly and change the emphasis or some part of what I was trying to do. What I didn't really account for were the times when he was just humoring me.

Imagine my surprise when I would move from a concept to implementation, only to find out I'd built my plans on a foundation of shifting sand. My boss, it turns out, liked to say "yes" to me in person, but sometimes wouldn't mean it. When he would talk to City Councilors, he would apparently forget that he was nodding at me the whole time I was talking.

I learned to "trust but verify," as Ronald Reagan once said about the Soviet Union. In the face of resistance from his bosses, he would not fight for what I thought was "our" idea. So, I had to do a little reconnaissance of my own to determine how deep his support was.

While I attribute a lot of that dynamic to a lack of management prowess on his part, I also take ownership of some of the blame. I also needed to make sure that he got the support he needed to go to his superiors and advance ideas. That means I had to make it easy for him. Where possible, I needed to provide relevant, compelling cases that he could send up the food chain. I also needed to remember to read the body language in the room. Sometimes support is only a nod when you are in the room.

What can you do to shore up your boss' support and make sure it doesn't end at the next box up in the power structure? How you approach this issue depends a lot on the dynamics of your workplace. Some alternative strategies include the following:

- *Having direct discussions up the organizational chart.* If your boss is not a very hierarchical person, it's worth lightening their load by doing some of the talking for them. If they don't have time to lobby for an issue, you may be able to take the time. However, it's critical to make sure this approach doesn't backfire, as it might do in a rigid power structure.
- *Planting ideas in the public realm.* If you have a chance to sell your idea in a context you know will get broad exposure, you can reach the entire power structure in your community at once. If you have chances to speak publicly—say at a Chamber of Commerce breakfast or a neighborhood association—use that as a chance to communicate with everyone in attendance. Explain your good ideas and why they make sense. If your boss was a soft supporter of them, it may shore their support up. More importantly, it may help you get the support of the final decision makers.
- *Sharing supportive material.* If something you want to do is a common practice elsewhere, make sure everyone knows that! Figure out ways to share supportive articles and news from similar communities. Find unbiased thinktanks and share links to their research. Leaders are far more willing to lead when they know someone else has taken similar actions before!

One note of caution—don't get too far ahead of your immediate boss. If they are not supportive of your ideas, taking any of these steps is risky at best and job-ending at worst. Make sure your support, while perhaps soft, is genuine!

The power dynamic is a complex and dangerous thing. I think of it like electrical work. If you know what you are doing, you can do wonderful things. If not, somewhere, lines will cross and you will either get shocked or make all the lights go out!

The Political Appointee and Your Office

We can't really complete this conversation until we tackle a big, rarely discussed issue in many public sector offices. Often, leading within these organizations is simply discouraged.

In fact, it can get you thrown out on the street.

In most public settings, there are the political leaders and the non-political managers. Political leaders are sometimes directly elected (such as a Mayor). In other situations, while they are still political leaders, they are not directly elected. They may be appointed by an elected official. For example, the State Department of Environmental Protection often has a "Secretary" who is really the boss. That person is often appointed by the Governor. A new Governor is elected, and the person sitting in that corner office is usually replaced by someone else.

Those political leaders are there to provide direction from the Governor down to professional staff. They may send a directive down to a planning office, for example, that the city is "open for business" or that "developers should pay their fair share." They will leave it to the Planning Director and their staff to figure out what that means. Do they change how they do business? If they don't, what will the consequences be?

In addition, those directives are sometimes coming down for a reason. It's fair to ask you, as a leader within such an organization, to take a deep look and see if there really are problems or issues. If there are, you should address them. If there aren't and the directive seems to you to be as much about show as about substance, it still makes sense to look closely at this issue and at least make some minor changes to try to address a perceived issue.

These political leaders are also there to ensure that the work done in the office is consistent with their views and interests—or those of their appointers. This could simply be described as quality control. Others might describe it as monitoring. If they asked your office to make sure that "developers pay their fair share," they may review staff reports to determine if the staff appear to be doing so. This can be challenging if the leader has limited experience in planning. That may leave it to you, as a professional, to explain how the process works.

Let's look at this issue from two perspectives. If you are that political appointee, how do you lead in an office where your leadership isn't entirely about good planning? On the other hand, if you are the highest non-political member of a planning department—say the career-track Deputy Director—how to do you manage what may be a regularly changing set of politically appointed department heads?

As a political appointee, you may or may not have any actual experience in the field in which you are asked to lead—in this case, planning. Let's assume that since you are reading this book, you have some background in the field. Perhaps you worked on a Governor's campaign because you liked his general viewpoint and electability, and when he was elected, he appointed you to head his state planning office. Suddenly you are wearing two hats.

Your boss, the Governor, has certain goals that are likely fairly generic when it comes to specific planning issues. Your professional background tells you what you think a state planning office should do. Finally, there are laws and regulations that govern what the office is supposed to do and how it is supposed to do it. These rules put strict guardrails around your activities in many respects.

This is a challenge. On the other hand, it's also a chance to show planning leadership in the highest sense. Balancing political expectations, good practice, and legal requirements is a three-dimensional game of chess of planning. Doing an excellent job in this position—and keeping the confidence of your boss—is the type of challenge great planning leaders relish.

Conversely, as Deputy Director who is not a political appointee, every few years you may be welcoming a new boss into the nice office next to yours. How do you advance your leadership agenda?

It's actually not as different a challenge as you may think. In this case, you also need to think somewhat politically. Your new boss knows they may not be in that position very long. They are likely to decide relatively quickly how much they can trust you to both do a good job and be a team player. Your challenge is to make sure your first few interactions with them create that bond of trust.

This may involve a number of strategies. One is to make sure you understand what's on your boss' to-do list. If they have been told to make sure all applicants are treated fairly, be prepared to be challenged as to whether your office is doing so. If they have idealistic expectations for getting people out of cars and into public transit, it's worth looking through the city code ahead of time and coming up with ideas as to how to do so with the existing processes. This will work best if, as described above, your interests and those of your boss align, at least to some extent. It will be more challenging if they don't.

Another strategy for getting in your boss' good graces is simply to play it straight, within reason. Keep in mind how they likely view the world, and explain good work you are doing in those terms. If there are common phrases in your staff's reports that you know will not be received well, see how to reword the message, if not the content.

The challenge in this type of Deputy Director role is more about how to *lead* than how to *manage*. How do you make sure your priorities don't get lost in your boss' priorities? That's the challenge you can tackle once you've made it past that first step of gaining their confidence.

You should bring your big ideas to your boss and explain why they are important for good professional practice. Don't sugarcoat the idea too much in political terms, though you should be prepared to explain why it's not a bad political move. You should explain that it is a good planning practice, explain why, and also have an informal explanation of why the idea won't be politically harmful. If they feel you are doing a good job on their key priorities, hopefully they will let you carve out some time for yours.

Working for a Living

Sometimes the way staff survive a political environment is to avoid conflict altogether. You have likely met someone who has followed this rule. A senior member of staff in your department—or another—may be technically competent and thorough, but generally unwilling to offer a strong opinion on an issue. As new political winds flow, that person may either bend in that direction or simply duck low and focus on day-to-day actions.

These are employees who are either simply focused on keeping their jobs or who believe in the administration of the rules more than their policy goals. If the policy goals change, either type of person will change with them.

This is not meant to disparage all managers who keep their nose to the grindstone and do all the everyday work. Not only is there an important role for such people, but they are also the true public servants who take care of the people's business. However, they are rarely leaders.

This is not an issue for you as a planning leader in most cases. These workers will work with you on almost anything they think is not going to irritate their bosses. If they are in other departments, they will look to their department heads in some cases, but will also generally work with you.

Where it does become an issue is when this sort of role becomes an impediment for you. You may be trying to work on a project that needs the assistance of another department, and the head of that department does not feel that the project's risk is worth the return. You may simply be surrounded by indifference, perhaps a sense that your priority is just another passing fad that isn't worth putting too much effort into.

This indifference is frustrating, especially if you are particularly excited about your ideas. You may have gone to the effort of getting the Mayor's signoff, only to find your project stalled by staff who just aren't that interested in it. They won't explicitly block it, but their fear of political ramifications is far deeper than your peak of excitement.

This challenge harks back to the discussion in Chapter 3 about managing your organization. Sometimes, it also has this political factor. In this case, you will have to let your staff know that you understand their reticence. It's important to let them know you've gone to the top of the organization to get approval. It's also worth suggesting that, now that you've received that approval, your success in this effort will reflect on the whole organization. If it works well, there's no real political downside.

Final Thoughts on Power

Workplace dynamics are complicated, especially in the environment most planners work in. If you are consulting, you may be part of a team working together on a project while various members are in a complex dance of partnership and rivalry while trying to pay the bills. If you are in government, people are motivated by various things in their work, usually based on their professional passions or a desire to survive until pension time. Power dynamics are shifting and unpredictable, and external stakeholders can sometimes drive the agenda.

You may not be entirely in charge of your organization, and that's OK. You should do what you can to advance good planning while remaining a trusted member of a team. Thinking through the complex web of relationships you have to navigate is an important part of achieving that goal.

5

LEADING PUBLIC OPINION

So, if you drive to work, what gives you the right to tell people to take the bus?

I was sweating. I was a young regional planner and believed deeply in how important transit is to a strong region. But it was a rural part of the country and spread out. I had tried to find an apartment near my office or on one of the limited bus lines that would get me there, but no luck. It is a seasonal area, with long sandy beaches and lighthouses, and the real money is in seasonal rentals. Year-round housing is hard to find.

When I finally found a year-round rental that I could afford, I gave up on my hope of walking to work and resigned myself to driving to work.

And now an aggressive reporter was asking me if that was hypocritical.

Lots of nuanced answers came to mind. The seasonal nature of the housing market making it hard to find a place to live. The challenge of providing good transit in a rural environment. The difference between professional advice and personal choices. But none of them seemed to matter at that moment as I sweated in front of a smart reporter.

Fortunately, this was just an exercise. After a moment, the "reporter" relaxed his shoulders and laughed. This was a media training exercise to help us young planners in responding to the media.

"I really had you there, didn't I?" he asked. He clearly had set a trap for me and I had walked right into it.

I admitted I had no idea how to answer. There's no reason I should have. I was trained in a traditional urban planning background. Lots of work on demographics, mapping tools, policy analysis, and urban design. Not a lot about how to deal with a public that doesn't understand why these issues matter. Definitely nothing on how to speak to reporters.

It doesn't matter how good your message is if you can't get someone to explain it well. Sometimes that person is you. Just as often, it's a reporter or neighborhood resident. Without getting your message out effectively and accurately, you're not leading the way in planning.

Good Leaders Are Good Communicators

Most people barely understand what planning is. They may think it's a variant on architecture, or engineering, or politics. I had a friend ask me if I was the one who decides how traffic lights change. None of that is entirely false, but it misses the point.

When people don't even know what you do, it's a challenge to help them understand why it matters. It's even harder to get them to understand why they should listen to you.

Think of a common issue that everyone has an opinion about: commuting. Many people commute, and they mostly drive. They want to get where they are going and get there quickly, and park close by. So, if they have problems doing so, they want planners to do something about it.

The good news there is that you have their attention. But they may not like what you have to say about it! If traffic is bad, they probably think the right answer is to widen the roads. If they can't park nearby, they probably want you to plan for more parking. While these solutions are sometimes part of good planning, often planners have legitimate concerns about providing more roads and parking.

Widened roads result in historic building torn down, additional air pollution, and impacts on urban design. Even worse, they often don't work. Widened roads often attract more traffic and end up as congested, with all the negative impacts mentioned above. Providing more parking can also have the opposite impact than was intended.

Planners often look to land use and multimodal solutions to traffic issues. Providing walkable communities, compatible land uses, and better transit and sidewalks are common solutions planners come up with when faced with congestion.

Those are not generally popular solutions. If the public doesn't like them, chances are the political leaders don't like them. That often means you're not implementing them.

So, what's a well-meaning planner with good ideas to do?

Get your message out!

This goes way beyond knowing how to speak to a reporter. Let's back up and start at the beginning.

Planning and the Rest of the World

Other than talking shop with your colleagues, most everything you say or do involves using communication skills. You probably understand this intuitively, but it's important to think that through. Whether it's speaking to a citizen who calls you up, concerned about a development nearby, or presenting a zoning change to a City Council, or speaking to a reporter, you need to use a different mindset and language than you probably learned in school.

There are a few different reasons why external communications are different:

- Most people don't speak "planner"—every discipline has its own language and acronyms, and planning is no exception. Telling a resident that a developer is allowed to use TDR in their PUD is a quick way to lose your message.
- Most people don't think about planning as much as you do—just like you may not spend a lot of time thinking about zoology, a zookeeper who lives on the same street as a new park under development is not going to have thought about it until they hear it means people will park on their street.
- It's public—while most things that planners do in the public sector are technically public, there's nothing as public as being quoted on

the evening news. In that case, you're lucky if you get 15 seconds to explain things, and even then, you may not get to choose the 15 seconds they use on the broadcast!

To a greater or lesser extent, these reasons apply everywhere outside of planning offices and conferences. Getting comfortable with them and using opportunities that you are offered is how to become an effective leader.

Mordecai Lee explains that public relations is a tool for doing better public administration. It implements the central mission of the organization and fulfills the democratic responsibilities of a government organization. Lee further divides public sector communications into three general categories (Lee 2012, 12–13):

1. *Mandatory.* These include media relations, public reporting, and responsiveness to the public. At its core, these are the most democratic reasons to be good at communication—because it's your job!
2. *Optional.* These include providing additional responsiveness to public (as customers and clients, not just citizens), increasing utilization of services and products, providing public education and public service campaigns, seeking voluntary compliance with laws and regulations, and using the public as extra eyes and ears of the agency. These are more pragmatic reasons to be a good communicator—these are not required, but they make you a better planner.
3. *"Dangerous, But Powerful"*—this area involves getting close to the line in advocating for your views and initiatives to increase public support. Proactively promoting your agenda can be unacceptable in some contexts and normal in others. While Lee sees these advocacy roles as controversial in public administration generally, they are less so in planning than in some areas of government. As a planner, you are expecting to have some opinions—it's just a question of how you advance them.

This framework is a good starting point to look at how you represent your organization. However, when you add in the goal of leading for excellent planning initiatives, it is helpful to factor in how often these interactions take place and compare that issue to how risky that external interaction is for you and your organization. Taking a phone call from a Planning Board member asking about a project is both low risk and routine. Yet, even those basic calls provide opportunities for leadership, as they give you a chance to explain how and why that project fits the larger planning goals of your organization.

On the other hand, it's easy to imagine a situation where you are promoting a change in zoning to more closely match the existing neighborhood. Neighborhood residents—also known as voters—are generally upset by this proposal because they don't want to see more development. You believe that there are opportunities for infill development in that neighborhood to help address housing needs, and even contributed to the streetscape by allowing vacant lots to be developed into new homes. You suspect that the Mayor and many Councilors won't support this effort, even if the Planning Board does. How do you try to get out your message there? Do you try at all?

Any actions on this effort—whether talking to a reporter on the background or connecting a Planning Board member with influential members of the local neighborhood group—are risky. Word could get back to your boss, the Mayor, that you were organizing on an issue she didn't support. This is an example of an effort that might be deliberate, but also risky.

There are also strategic efforts. These are more long term and are not focused on short-term results. One example might be to decide to have a public meeting about parking in the downtown area. There's no specific effort on the table, no code changes actively being proposed. However, you are trying to get a discussion going about an important issue, and educate the public about the tradeoffs between providing more parking and offering alternatives such as better transit and walkability. Such an effort might be risky or not, depending on the political dynamic over this issue.

Finally, there are incidental opportunities for outreach and messaging. These are the least predictable and may happen at a moment's notice. For example, you walk into a downtown building and step into an elevator, only to discover that the city's largest landowner—and longtime critic of planning—is the only other person in the elevator. What do you say to him? Is this a chance to find some common ground on something? How risky is it to say anything substantive at all?

Each of these activities has a part to play in making positive change. Each of them is easy and hard for various types of people. In general, your comfort level is somewhat correlated to where you work. Local

Table 5.1 Ways to influence public opinion by risk level and type of activity

	Routine	Deliberate	Strategic	Incidental
Low Risk	Phone call from a resident		Putting out Department Updates on Twitter	Conversation with an influence leader in the elevator
Medium Risk	Explaining something to a reporter	Managing your message		
Risky	Presenting to City Council	Outlining rationale of new parking waivers to a reporter	Explaining new parking waivers on a Facebook page	

government planners tend to prefer the low-risk and routine. Nonprofit and community-based planners tend toward the risky and strategic. That's in part because, for them, it's not risky. In fact, not speaking their mind can actually be riskier, as their whole model is based on changing the current paradigm.

We're mostly looking at local government here, so this model generally holds. How should we approach each of these activities effectively and—dare I say it—safely?

Customer Service

The phone rings—or more often now, you get a new email in your inbox. You may even get a social media posting. Regardless of how you receive it, someone is asking you for information.

You want to help—at least, you should want to help! Even if that person isn't your favorite resident. Even if that person dislikes you and is convinced you are trying to ruin their neighborhood. You should almost always want to help. The question is what does it mean to help?

This is a "low-risk," "routine" effort in the model discussed. Even so, it's not without some risks, and it's not always routine:

- *Treat them respectfully.* Even if they don't treat you well, you need to start by taking the high road. You shouldn't yell back (or use the equivalent ALL CAPS in writing). There is no need to take the bait if they

make disparaging comments. Respond as helpfully as you can. If the person isn't actually asking you for information, but is simply making accusations or implying your guilt in some activity, you may not need to respond at all. Sometimes a brief "thanks for your thoughts" says more than not responding at all, as you have then taken the high road.
- *Respond in a timely fashion.* Most planning offices don't have a standard operating procedure related to response time. Nonetheless, you should try to respond to all your inquiries within a few days. If you will need more time for an accurate response, you can say so and buy yourself more time. In general, the "touch time" on inquiries should be within a few days—if it is longer than that, some people assume you aren't responding and may start telling others you ignored them.
- *Feel free to direct people rather than answer them.* If your office has a decent online portal with information about projects, you don't need to gather that data for them. You can simply send along a link to that portal with some instructions. Having a standard email response that says that saves a lot of time. There may be times when you take the extra effort to pull that data yourself. That may make sense when you know residents struggle with computers or are particularly sensitive. But that sort of analysis is fading into some of the other forms of communication we will discuss later.
- *Don't blame someone for being upset.* Lots of what you work on every day is controversial and most people who contact you are not well versed in planning issues. They most likely heard about a new project or plan, sometimes in a negative or alarming way, and start from a position of concern. Providing a human face to your role in that process is important. Offer to explain the process. Answer questions clearly and without bias. Don't seem impatient, even if you are.

Customer service is a concept that has been applied more frequently to public offices in recent years. Much of the standard training on private sector customer service applies—but not all of it. Your customers are not like retail customers. They may not want to be working with your office. They may just want you and what you are working on to go away. That's not the attitude they usually take when going into their favorite store.

Your customer service should be as informed by the way an insurance claim line acts as a luxury restaurant. Both require good people skills, but the people ended up there for very different reasons.

Customer Service—Routine/Low Risk

The conventional wisdom is that public agencies should look at people who come into their office as customers. That's generally true. But not all customers are the same. As with private organizations, there are many customers who have come to transact, and need to be provided with clear information and easy systems to get things done. However, like private organizations, there are customers who are not "always right."

While not a public agency (or maybe for that reason), it's helpful to look at L.L. Bean. The internationally renowned maker of boots, flannel, and other soft goods has long been known for its excellent customer service. If something is wrong, it wants to make it right. That's as a good company—or a good public organization—should be.

However, L.L. Bean had a problem. Like the teacher who was always willing to give students better grades if they complained, L.L. Bean was allowing too many returns. It had a long-standing policy of allowing any item it sold be returned at any time if a customer was not completely satisfied. That worked well when applied as intended. You didn't need a receipt or date of sale—just bring back your duck boot with the damaged sole and tell them you want to return it. However, this policy also had unintended consequences. People started buying old L.L. Bean items at thrift stores for pennies on the dollar and returning them to L.L. Bean. People who had actually bought items took them back long after their function life was over. What's an organization looking to have a good relationship with its customers supposed to do in that situation?

There's a lot of legitimate debate about using the term "customer" for users of city services. Clearly, residents who come into the City Clerk's to get a birth certificate or taxpayers who go to the Treasurer's Office to pay a bill are customers of city services. However, how do you classify people who come in to visit your office if not as "customers?" Sometimes private companies have unwilling customers too! Think of the people going to L.L. Bean to return defective clothes, and then find they have to wait behind all the thrift store opportunists. Don't they have a right to be served quickly and professionally? So should your applicants and even people complaining about your work.

One last thought on customer service: you will notice I mentioned above that "almost everyone" deserves a response. There are exceptions. Inquiries that are repetitive, get increasingly negative, or are threatening need to be handled differently. In general, I use the rule that every inquiry deserves a response and then a second response if a follow-up question arises. Then it depends on the nature of the conversation. If the inquiries seem legitimate and offer a chance to explain your process or how you view an issue, a good back-and-forth may be helpful. If the inquiries get increasingly negative and seem more like claims rather than questions, you can often end the back-and-forth once it's no longer helpful. My third email in these sorts of back-and-forth is often a simple "Thanks for your thoughts."

Finally, there are inquiries that go beyond that level and become simply threatening. Threats are not to be taken lightly in public offices, where there are few locks on doors or limits on who comes in. If you become at all concerned, consult with public safety. Sometimes your safety is more important than responding to someone who is implying violence, or worse.

Working with the Media: Routine/Medium Risk

Almost certainly, at some point in your planning career, you will have to speak to a reporter. How that happens depends on many factors—how public your position is; what your organization's media policy is; and how controversial your projects are. In the end, most planners end up on the other end of a reporter's phone line—or, as is more often the case today, email.

It's tempting to do the minimum when speaking to a reporter. It's safe to provide "just the facts": schedules, processes, and ordinances. When you get away from those areas, you enter a murky area where your words may be taken out of context. However, you also start to have a chance to show some leadership by explaining not just the "how," but the "why."

Once you decide to explain "why" to a reporter, it's critical to think about how reporters think. Frequently, they are not experts in planning. Even if one happens to specialize in the issue, much of their job is to explain things to readers, who almost certainly don't understand subdivision law, Community Development Block Grants, or fiscal policy. So it's critical to think critically about what you say and how you say it.

Speak in plain English!

If you use acronyms—and avoid them whenever possible—you need to spell them out. If you must explain something complicated, it's likely not worth the effort. Keep things at a high level and focused on why your work is important to the future. Be prepared for pushback and cynical responses. If you support affordable housing development, be prepared to answer questions about density and quality of life. If you support environmental protection, be prepared to answer questions about property rights.

It might seem like you can't win. You're not trying to win. You're trying to get the reporter to publish your message. The reporter wants to make your message seem controversial. Don't give them the space to do so.

While there are entire books written about media relations, here are a few key tips.

First, sometimes less is more. You don't have to answer every question you are asked. You should always give factual and complete information about what is happening, when, and what the public's chances to comment are. However, you don't always have to offer an opinion on everything you are asked. Pick one or two opinions you want included in each story and stick to them. Exert discipline and resist the instinct to chat.

Second, practice what you are going to say. Write down your talking points and stick to them as much as possible.

Third, you will get a sense after a while as to which reporters are more likely to understand and be interested in your message. Those are the reporters you can go off the record with and explain issues in more detail and with more opinions.

Fourth—and this is almost the opposite of the third point given above—television interviews are a great chance to get your message out. Television news almost always just want a three-second quote from you. Give them one or two, but make sure they represent what you want to tell the world. They will almost always use one of them.

Finally, as someone who has received my share of public records requests, I would recommend you develop a good document management system. Whether you use good old-fashioned paper or have moved to the cloud, keeping public documents in good order and handy is important for your reputation as a straight shooter. Part of that process involves determining which documents are not public. That doesn't mean they are secret, it just means they aren't part of the public record. Consult with your attorneys about what the public records laws are in your place of work. Any documents that don't need to be kept should, at a minimum, be stored separately from your public documents. For example, if you run a housing rehabilitation program, your recipients' financial data is probably not public. That should not be kept with the files that describe the program, how much you spent, and other public reporting elements.

Managing Your Message ("Inside the Lines"): Deliberate/Medium Risk

Being a leader in planning requires managing the routine activities well. However, it also requires more. Yes, you need to be able to quickly and clearly explain processes, but you also sometimes need to explain the why as much as the what. "Why" do you have a Planning Board review process? "Why" is it important to look at city plans and policies when a development site is examined?

Moving toward a more "deliberate" and "medium-risk" effort moves you beyond management and into leadership.

Of course, this is where your leadership risks coming into conflict with the political leadership of your government organization (or, for those of you in the private sector, the strategic goals of your organization). It's important to find areas where your message is most in line with the message of other leaders, and focus on those areas. Like many parts of leadership, it never hurts to be strategic.

Assuming you can resolve that challenge and find issues you would like to promote that are in keeping with the general direction of your organization, you can move from "if" to "how."

Imagine you are invited to speak before the local chamber of commerce. The topic is the permitting process. As with most chambers, the concern of the members is the time it takes to get approved and about uncertainty and cost. You've been asked to speak about this issue—and what *you* are doing to make it better.

This is an issue you have been working on in your time with the city. However, there are good reasons why the process takes the time it takes. Part of it is legal requirements such as advertising for hearings. Part of it is the fact that applicants rarely complete their applications completely. Another part of it is the natural back-and-forth that happens with applicants and staff on design issues, traffic, and other issues that need to be resolved. These issues are precisely the reason the process exists at all.

Your comprehensive plan outlines the importance of these issues to the health of your city. Your ordinances provide more details to implement those policies.

On the other hand, some of the staff in your office do sometimes go too far. In the course of their review, they sometimes focus on what a proposed development does wrong—and they don't always think about the positive benefits you bring to the community. That is a frustration you've had as the leader of the office, and one you are working on internally. You've made some progress.

One more detail about this chamber meeting: the Mayor is also speaking. You don't report directly to her, but she leads the City Council and you know that permitting times were one of her top campaign issues.

She speaks before you and talks sweepingly about how permits take too long in your city. She credits you for taking the issue seriously, but mostly emphasizes how much more there is to do in order to streamline the process.

You are not so sure. The process takes some time for good reasons. There are many residents who feel it's too fast and doesn't allow time to react. There are benefits from the process, in terms of better-planned developments and a more livable city. You rarely deny a project outright; you just work to improve them.

You're up next! What do you say?

Before you answer, think through the situation. It's important not to completely undermine and disagree with the Mayor, even if she isn't your direct boss. On the other hand, it's important to be somewhat honest, both for professional and ethical reasons. How do you thread that needle?

It never hurts to admit a little fault, even if you're not sure it's deserved. It builds goodwill and can help others admit some culpability. A planning leader should approach the situation with a response like this:

The issue of permitting time is complicated. On the city side, we have been guilty of sometimes losing perspective and not seeing the forest for the trees. I've worked with staff to focus on the big issues on a project, especially if it's one that has other benefits for the city. Part of the problem here is that our ordinance has been written in a way that makes it hard to approve anything! The rules are simply too hard to meet. We now meet weekly to review the status of permits and try to move them forward whenever possible.

On the other hand, we have also had problems with applicants not bothering to do their part. The easiest way to review an application is to have a complete application. I know that our current applications are excessively complicated and detailed. Your staff are working to simplify them. However, there is important information we need to review projects. If developers and their agents do their part to make their applications clear and complete, that helps us review them quickly.

I hope that, with all parties working towards a faster outcome, we can make the permitting process do what it is designed to do—make projects that meet city policies and plans—and not act as a barrier to good development.

This may not get a great reaction, but it is unlikely to alienate the Mayor or the Chamber. In fact, it may actually help!

Social Media (Strategic/Low to High Risk)

If there's one term that will probably seem dated in 20 years, it's "social media." If you doubt it, think of other terms like "Web 2.0" that were once used to describe similar tools.

Whatever you call it, interactive Web-based tools are here to stay. Increasingly, using them is not optional for planners. However, using social media as a planning tool is not as simple as liking someone's video of a dancing dog. In addition, with public noticing and records laws not keeping pace, the rules of engagement are not clear. They also change regularly.

It wasn't that long ago that Planning Board meetings were, at best, recorded on a City Hall audiovisual system. Recordings could be kept or burned onto DVDs, but were hard to come by. If you watched it, you could perhaps catch it on your local access cable channel as well. More recently, they may have been livestreamed on a specialized website and maybe archived.

Now, the baseline is that these meetings are available all those ways and may be seen on Facebook Live or Twitter feeds as well. Live time comments appear, and there is some expectation from those commenters that they may get responses. All this is in addition to your base job of providing the Board with good information and recommendations.

Even before the meeting, times have changed. Meetings used to be posted in a City Clerk's office and a city webpage. They now get pushed out on feeds, and if you don't post the actual agenda, there is a good change that someone else will post an item in order to bring a crowd to your meeting. While that's generally good for democracy, there is a risk that the posting party does not get the facts right, or the time, or whether public comment is even taken at that meeting.

In short, having a social media strategy is no longer optional for planning leaders; it's expected. The good news is that you don't have to go crazy and spent your entire evening keeping up with the latest platforms and memes. You just need to think this through and develop a plan that meets your needs, your willingness to take it beyond your needs, and the (reasonable) expectations of your constituents.

Developing a Social Media Strategy

As you develop a plan to use social media, think about a few factors:

- what you *need* to do;
- what you *want* to do; and
- what you *have time* to do.

You have some things you are either required to do legally or are expected to do based on your organizational culture. Getting those things done should be the top priorities. It's never effective to buck those cultural expectations. These actions, done well, are low risk and strategic. You may think they don't help you, but they build a sense of organizational competence. If you have staff who do these activities for you, think about

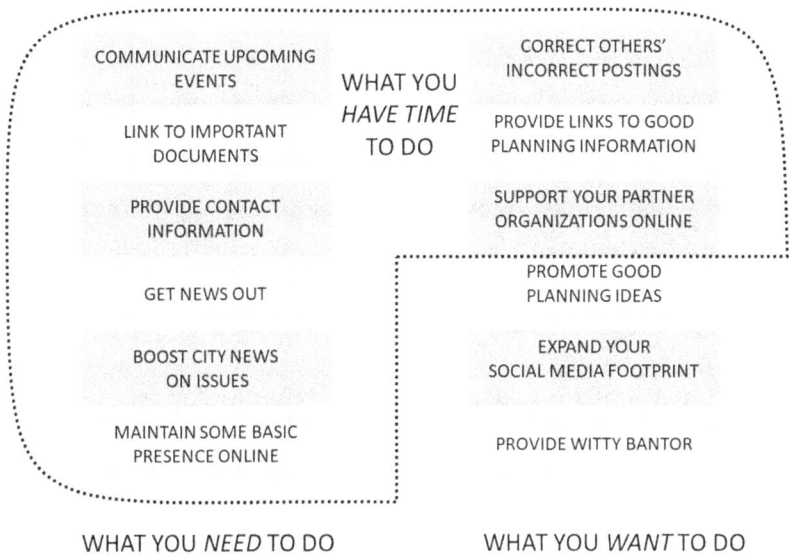

Figure 5.1 Figuring out what you need to do, what you'd like to do, and what you have time to do. Credit: Author.

ways to confirm they are being done on time and accurately. If your staff fail, you are the one whose image suffers!

You also see the potential for increasing your visibility and promoting good planning by pushing out important planning ideas and best practices. That's a laudable goal, but one that is not without risk. You must ensure that the ideas you promote don't conflict with the policy direction of political leaders. You also need to make sure your timing is correct. Don't post a link about transit use while your organization is mulling over a major change in its transit policies.

Finally, don't overstep your ability to do a good job on social media. If you open a social media account for your organization, you need to be able to keep it current. Posting on it once a week is a bare minimum. More importantly, you will get comments and messages from each account and will need to respond quickly. That's the point of social media. So consider picking one or two platforms you can manage responsibly. For example, I have used Twitter and Instagram, but decided that my office could not maintain an active presence on other platforms. However, many of our meetings are streamed on the city's Facebook page.

You don't have to have a social media presence. If you do, you don't have to be on every platform. Most importantly, if you do, commit yourself to doing a good job. Make sure you know what your organization's social media policies are. Remember that it's not your platform, it's the platform for your organization. Avoid politics—focus on facts and data. If you keep these ideas in mind, social media can help your organizational mission and your role as a leader.

Representing Your Organization: All the Time

Like it or not, you are a community leader already. You represent your organization and for many residents of your area, you speak for it at all times. Even at the supermarket. Buying ice cream. At two in the morning.

You're walking down the frozen foods aisle and walk into the local blogger, who loves to post semi-accurate statements about the latest developments, along with speculation as to who paid off who to get them approved. If anyone is paying anyone for these decisions, you're not aware of it. You're certainly not collecting any of it.

"It's you! I have a few questions about that new hotel that went in downtown. Can you confirm that at least two of members of the Planning Board were seen at dinner with the developer the week before their hearing? Isn't that embarrassing?"

What's really embarrassing for you is that you are wearing your flannel pants and someone recognized you. Mostly you just want to go home.

There are some strategies for avoiding these situations. Many planners choose not to live in the community in which they work. However, even they may find that moment at a gas station where the guy behind the counter recognizes you and wants to talk about that new subdivision going in.

"I live down the hill from it, and now I get water in my basement every time it rains! Didn't anyone think about that?" he asks you, as you pay for your gas and a Gatorade.

In fact, there were several studies done at the time. The developer is putting in a natural wetland to help with that issue, but it's not complete yet. There's a lot you could say about this issue to at least answer his question. On the other hand, you're late for picking your kids up at daycare.

Either way, you're in a situation where you are being asked to lead on a planning issue and you are not at all prepared. There are two legitimate ways to handle this situation:

1. Point out that you are actually not at work right then and offer to have them call you on Monday morning. The advantage of this approach is that you will get home quickly. The disadvantage is that you have lost the opportunity to provide accurate information and protect the integrity of your organization.
2. Spend some time engaging in a debate. The advantage of this approach is showing that you are not a 9 to 5 employee and that you care enough about the community to engage on these issues at any time. The disadvantage is that your ice cream might melt or you may have to pay a late fee to your childcare provider.

Deciding between these two approaches is tricky. You may not have to make the same choice every time you interact out-of-hours. Regardless, it's important to remember that people see you as the leader of your organization at all times, and that's part of having some leadership opportunities. If you are up for it, it's an opportunity to support your organization's efforts.

Working with the Press

How much you work with the media depends a lot on your exact situation. Anyone interested in leading in planning will likely have some contact. How you use that connection to both provide accurate information, and relay your message at the same time, is critical to your success.

Of course, nowadays the "press" is more than just newspapers. TV stations, bloggers, and even active group email lists all play a role in the modern media. While they should all be handled a little differently, there are some basic ideas to remember:

- *Be honest.* This may go without saying, but everything you say should be true. This doesn't mean you need to offer additional information that may be taken out of context. For example, you should tell a reporter if a project is on the agenda for next week and generally how likely it is that they may vote on it. You don't need to offer speculation about how they will vote or advocate for a particular position on the project. You definitely shouldn't use the media to pressure an independent board.

- *Answer with your message.* While you should generally answer the media's questions, you should always use these answers as a chance to convey what you want to say. Starting answers with "As outlined in the master plan for that area…" offers you a chance to showcase your good work and put decisions into context.
- *Remember the use.* While a trade journal may get into the weeds on your issue, a TV reporter is looking for one good soundbite. Give the appropriate answer. Don't say lots of things that may not work for the intended use. For example, if you know you will get one quote in a large article, develop one catchy phrase that conveys accurate and compelling information in plain English. Feel free to repeat it several times. Don't drift off-topic, as you then risk becoming the story based on something you said out of context!
- *The media is your friend.* Even if you get some bad stories, remember that the media is critical to a free and democratic society. You hopefully don't have anything too bad to hide. Be happy that there are people who are paid to make sure other public officials stay honest!
- *Keep it simple…* You know how this phrase ends. Don't use acronyms. Use the opportunity to explain how your processes work and why they are good. If they are not, use this as an opportunity to explain what you are trying to change.
- *Don't step on any feet.* Let the politicians get the credit when possible. You don't need to be in competition with them. Similarly, it never hurts to credit your boss for a good idea or for encouraging you to look at a best practice.

Working with Boards

Many, if not most, planning leaders work with public boards and commissions. Whether a Planning Board, a Zoning Board of Appeals, or even a City Council, you are likely working with people who are either elected or appointed. Most likely they are not professional planners. Hopefully, when they want planning advice, they will look to you.

I hate to tell you, but those boards will not always follow your advice. They are not designed to, and getting irritated at them is simply a waste of energy. All you can do is provide them with solid, well-explained recommendations and hope they take them into account.

On the other hand, don't just shrug your shoulders. How and when you work to convince these boards of your veracity is a key part of planning leadership. Your memos should be concise and persuasive. You should think about counter-arguments and provide responses proactively. As with the media, don't use jargon or acronyms. Most likely, many members of these boards will rotate out and you will have to get used to explaining planning ideas to a new audience.

While the well-drafted memo is important, it's also important to get along with board members on a personal level. It's much easier for them to agree with you if they like you. So spend time cultivating those relationships. If it's a board you work with a lot and manage, consider an annual picnic or Christmas dinner. Have check-in calls with the board chair ahead of time if you can. Even if your relationship is more distant, as it may be with a City Council, there's nothing wrong with some friendly social talk with members in the hall about sports, kids, or whatever interests you both.

You do need to be careful. This is a professional relationship and, at the end of the day, the board member is the one with more authority than you. You should just make sure you keep in mind that you are not hanging out with a college friend. Some places even have rules about what you can and can't discuss outside of a public meeting. However, in the end, there's nothing wrong with being friendly!

The Balancing Act

Public opinion is critical to getting good planning done. It's important to use your experiences speaking publicly as opportunities to give out good information, but also to occasionally explain a good planning concept or technique. You are most likely the leader in planning issues in your community.

It's important to remember that the best work is done behind the scenes. While you want to be consistent as a voice for good planning, it is the political leaders who can get much of your agenda implemented. Keeping a good, cordial relationship with them provides an opportunity for your ideas to become their ideas. True leadership means sometimes you give credit to others!

Maintaining a professional office with competent staff is also an important part of being heard. That quiet competence means something about you and your integrity. Similarly, having good customer service skills, which is important in itself, is also a way to gain opportunities for advancing your ideas.

You also need to remember when not to push an idea. There are times when the political winds aren't right or you need to focus on the basic operations of your office. There may even be times when you are forced to clean up a major public relations debacle. These are not the times to advance important issues.

LOOKING THROUGH A POLICY WINDOW

It seems like there should never be a bad time for a good idea. In reality, however, there are many more bad times for a good idea than the rare good one. As a planning leader, you need to look at the external environment and figure out when there may be that opportunity to advance a good idea, rather than just choosing a time for your own convenience.

When does an opportunity to advance a good idea happen? These "policy windows" generally open when a problem is exposed and people are looking for solutions. For example, planners have been advocating for years for the use of parking spaces for outdoor dining opportunities. The idea of using so-called "parklets" to expand the vitality of downtowns is supported by many planners and is opposed by many who are concerned about the loss of parking, or the perception that these spaces are dirty, dangerous, and incompatible with the street. While some cities have advanced parklet dining spaces, the idea has stalled in many others.

Figure 5.2 A "parklet" in Portland, ME. Credit: Author

With the arrival of the COVID-19 pandemic in 2020, the idea of al fresco dining took on a whole new importance. Restaurants were not allowed to serve indoors and many people didn't want to go inside spaces due to concerns about getting sick. At the same time, parking demand was way down in most cities, because of the closure of many stores and offices. For the first time, many elements aligned and a policy window opened to allow these parklet spaces in many cities. The concerns of local restaurants, planners, and residents all pushed in the same direction rather than in conflicting ways.

The result? Lots of parklets all over the country. Whether they will be permanent or not, everyone will have a chance to try them out now, and see what concerns are real and what concerns were just unjustified worry.

Bibliography

Lee, Mordecai. 2012. "Government Public Relations: What Is It Good For?" In Mordecai Lee et al. (eds), *The Practice of Government Public Relations*. Boca Raton, FL: CRC Press, Taylor & Francis Group, 9–25.

6

LEADING BY LISTENING

In 1965, planning had a growing problem. Lots of people hated planning—and planners!

This was not without cause. We've talked a lot about the excesses of urban renewal and how planners alienated communities. There was also the problem of the American instinct against centralized planning. Americans liked it when planning meant protecting the value of their home—at least the Americans who were lucky enough to own a home—but that really isn't the main purpose of planning. In addition to some self-inflicted wounds, there was the the general discontent of the 1960s. As a result, the profession of planning was in trouble.

Some planners turned to Jane Jacobs and focused on the concept of allowing cities to develop on their own. Again, this raised the question of whether that is really the core goal of planning.

Others regarded the entire profession as rotten to the core. No doubt there were some planners who left the profession during that period. No doubt there were also planners who sought refuge in the federal agencies that continued large-scale projects. Building interstates and financing subdivisions was far removed from the day-to-day interactions at which planners were apparently bad.

Into this context came Paul Davidoff. A lawyer and city planner by training, Davidoff was born in New York City in 1930 and no doubt was influenced by the urban renewal projects advanced by Robert Moses and his peers. As a graduate student at the University of Pennsylvania, he was also likely exposed to Edmund Bacon's slightly mellower—but still top-heavy—methods of planning.

Davidoff had a very different view of planning. He believed that planners were doing it all wrong. Instead of telling communities how they should be planned, he believed that planners needed to listen to their needs and then become a voice for the public in decision making. At the same time, he proposed that planners should bring their own values of inclusiveness and positive change to the table in order to support residents' needs.

In *The City Reader*, Richard LeGates and Frederic Stout summarize Davidoff's view on planning, and how it emerges somewhat from his legal background:

> Like a lawyer, the advocate planner's role is to serve her client, not the public at large. The advocate planner leaves it to competing advocate planners to represent other interests, just as lawyers in legal cases leave it to opposing counsel to argue the other side of a legal case. In Davidoff's proposed model of planning, the local planning commissioners would be confronted with different proposed plans and would be forced to weigh the merits of the competing plans much as a court weighs competing evidence and opposing legal arguments in a legal case presented by competing lawyers. The planning commissioners would make the ultimate decisions about a plan's contents, somewhat like judges decide the outcome in legal cases, but would have more discretion to pick and choose parts of the plans presented to them.
>
> Davidoff believed plans that would emerge from such a process would be better than plans prepared by planning department staff without the interplay of competing advocacy planners. The justification for adversarial systems has been well developed by legal theorists. Law professors point out that conflict keeps people honest.

It makes lawyers work hard because they know that their work will be critically scrutinized. And it gives judges competing points of view supported by evidence from which to choose. Davidoff reasoned that the needs of the poor and powerless would be better met in city plans if—a big if—they were adequately represented by advocacy planners speaking on their behalf. Davidoff was particularly concerned with low-income minority communities. (LeGates and Stout 2020, 480–481)

This concept, known as "advocacy planning," changed the field forever. Barry Checkoway, writing in the *Journal of the American Planning Association* in 1994, summed up Davidoff's worldview well:

Davidoff viewed planning as a process to promote democratic pluralism in society, by representing diverse groups in political debate and public policy. Pluralism would stimulate city planning, he argued, by better informing the public of alternative choices, and by forcing the planning agency to compete with other groups for political support.

Davidoff challenged planners to become advocates "for what they deemed proper" and for their client's vision of "the good society." He urged planners to express their values, engage openly in the political process, and help groups to formulate their plans and develop their capacity. He viewed advocacy as a way of enabling all groups in society, and singled out "organizations representing low-income families" as especially important: "The plans prepared for these groups would seek to combat poverty and would propose programs affording new and better opportunities to the members of the organization and to families similarly situated." (Checkoway 1994, 140–141)

Davidoff worked for much of his career to advance these concepts, even running for Congress at one point. He founded the Suburban Action Institute in 1969, which brought forward the groundbreaking *South Burlington County NAACP v. Mount Laurel Township* case in New Jersey, arguing successfully that every community must do their "fair share" to provide for below-market affordable housing.

However, most importantly to planners, he changed the paradigm of what it meant to plan. In 1965, the *Journal of the American Institute of Planners* published his article "Advocacy and Pluralism in Planning" (Davidoff 1965), which crystallized his view of the profession and how it must change to remain relevant.

Davidoff believed that planners should not just worry about how buildings look or how they are laid out in a city. Instead, they should look to the residents and promote their interests. The planner was part-advocate and part-technical advisor who could help advance the needs of the public by taking their visions and turning them into strategies. Those strategies, he felt, were the responsibility of the planner to push in the political process:

> The advocate planner would be responsible to his client and would seek to express his client's views. This does not mean that the planner could not seek to persuade his client. In some situations persuasion might not be necessary, for the planner would have sought out an employer with whom he shared common views about desired social conditions and the means toward them. In fact one of the benefits of advocate planning is the possibility it creates for a planner to find employment with agencies holding values close to his own. Today the agency planner may be dismayed by the positions affirmed by his agency, but there may be no alternative employer.
>
> The advocate planner would be above all a planner. He would be responsible to his client for preparing plans and for all of the other elements comprising the planning process. Whether working for the public agency or for some private organization, the planner would have to prepare plans that take account of the arguments made in other plans. Thus the advocate's plan might have some of the characteristics of a legal brief. It would be a document presenting the facts and reasons for supporting one set of proposals, and facts and reasons indicating the inferiority of counterproposals. The adversary nature of plural planning might, then, have the beneficial effect of upsetting the tradition of writing plan proposals in terminology which makes them appear self-evident.
>
> A troublesome issue in contemporary planning is that of finding techniques for evaluating alternative plans. Technical devices such as cost–benefit analysis by themselves are of little assistance

without the use of means for appraising the values underlying plans. Advocate planning, by making more apparent the values underlying plans, and by making definitions of social costs and benefits more explicit, should greatly assist the process of plan evaluation. Further, it would become clear (as it is not at present) that there are no neutral grounds for evaluating a plan; there are as many evaluative systems as there are value systems.

The adversary nature of plural planning might also have a good effect on the uses of information and research in planning. One of the tasks of the advocate planner in discussing the plans prepared in opposition to his would be to point out the nature of the bias underlying information presented in other plans. In this way, as critic of opposition plans, he would be performing a task similar to the legal technique of cross-examination. While painful to the planner whose bias is exposed (and no planner can be entirely free of bias) the net effect of confrontation between advocates of alternative plans would be more careful and precise research.

Not all the work of an advocate planner would be of an adversary nature. Much of it would be educational. The advocate would have the job of informing other groups, including public agencies, of the conditions, problems, and outlook of the group he represented. Another major educational job would be that of informing his clients of their rights under planning and renewal laws, about the general operations of city government, and of particular programs likely to affect them. (Davidoff 1965, 333)

In many languages, the word "lawyer" resembles the word "advocate." In Davidoff's case, he saw a significant overlap between the roles of the two professions.

So what does this mean for the planner? Should you get a law degree? Not necessarily. But you need to think of the planner as a conduit for public sentiment, with a value-added component. For example, the average resident of most communities will think it's hard to park downtown. When you ask her why she won't go downtown, she may say she doesn't want to deal with finding parking. She may remember getting a parking ticket for overstaying her time at a meter, or a time when she was running late and just couldn't find a space.

Does that mean your job as a planner is to go out and advocate for more parking downtown? It may. However, there is a great deal of planning research that suggests that the issue is more complex than it may seem to the typical non-planner. Often the problem is not that parking is too scarce, but that it is too cheap. If you can park for free all day in front of a business, that space is not likely to be available for a short stop into that business. If it costs a reasonable amount, it will turn over frequently and be available for someone who needs it.

Similarly, sometimes the problem is too much parking. Many downtowns tore down many old buildings over time to create more parking. That may result in sufficient parking for those downtowns, but not enough things to do downtown to make it worth going there. There's a reason why places people want to go often have parking challenges—they didn't eliminate buildings with interesting things in them and replace them with parking.

It's the role of the planner—especially the planner who wants to lead—to have that conversation with the resident and explain the research. You may not get her full agreement, but you are adding value to the conversation. You can then go forward into the public debate and explain that the residents want to make it easier to get downtown, and that a solution involves a number of planning tools. One of those may be to build a new parking lot—but perhaps as part of a set of initiatives.

In short, you are not just a conduit for public sentiment. On the other hand, it's important to hear what residents have to say and then process that input with your expertise.

THE CHALLENGE OF ADVOCATING FOR OTHERS

Most planners have had an experience where a project they think addresses a local need—say for housing, or job creation, or even a new bike path—encounters resistance. You watch the emails and letters pile up as you prepare the staff report, almost entirely opposed to the project. As you finalize the package to go with your report, you are faced with the fact that you are planning to recommend support for the project, while the package will include a large number of community voices disagreeing with you.

> Why do you do this? Sometimes it may be as simple as you knowing that the project meets all the standards in code for approval. In that case, it's not a popularity contest—if the project meets the standards, it should be approved.
>
> In other cases, you know that there is a real need for the project and that those who support it are less likely to contact you to express their views. For one thing, many people don't know how the approval process works. Others may not have the time, or access to a computer, or may simply be distracted by the daily pressures of life. Sometimes, possible supporters may not even be aware of the project. In any case, it's generally true that people are far more likely to write in opposition to a project as they are in support of one.
>
> If you are supporting a project where the record shows broad opposition, you may be implementing a form of advocacy planning. You may have spoken to people who expressed the need for such a project. You may simply have data that shows they exist. In any case, you are sticking your professional neck out for others.
>
> You get to the hearing and it gets even worse. The opponents to the project hold a rally in front of City Hall before the meeting. They come into the room with stickers and you can tell they have read your report and are not happy with you. Opponents testify for two hours on detailed reasons why the project should be denied. You may be lucky if a few people come in support as well.
>
> These are trying times to be a planner. On the other hand, these are also sometimes times when your professional ethics require that you advocate for those who are not there. In the long run, it's worth thinking about how to get some supporters to these meetings in the future. For now, however, you are alone.

Institutionalizing Advocacy Planning

I suspect that those of you who are practicing municipal planners are aware of these concepts and see some of them in your everyday work. However, much of your experience (or at least mine) is likely to be a patchwork of methods and processes, sometimes touching on these ideas and sometimes not. Did the ideas from Davidoff ever really get incorporated into a planning process from the ground up?

Yes. In Cleveland! Thanks to the leadership of Norman Krumholz, who led the planning efforts there for much of the 1970s.

Krumholz was a planning leader of the highest sort. He not only had a clear vision of how he wanted to make change in the world, but he apparently also had the strategic ability (and perhaps good luck) to work with political leaders who supported him. He became City Planning Director of Cleveland in 1969, under Mayor Carl Stokes.

Stokes, an interesting leader himself, was elected Mayor of Cleveland in 1967 as the first elected African-American mayor of a major American city. His election was no sure thing, as he ran against Seth Taft, a member of the long-standing Ohio Taft political family. Narrowly defeating Taft, Stokes went on to lead Cleveland for four years. His time as Mayor was a time of community engagement and activist city government, so it's not entirely surprising that Krumholz and Stokes were pulling in the same direction.

Krumholz was a believer in advocacy planning and the re-invention of the profession. Rather than developing physical plans for the city, he promoted the idea of "policy plans" that put forward ways in which cities should advance goals. Instead of drawing a new streetscape, his plans described how to make a better streetscape happen. The introduction to the 1975 "Cleveland Policy Planning Report" stated as follows:

> The pages that follow outline the Cleveland City Planning Commission's recommendations for resolving or ameliorating some of the most pressing problems confronting the City of Cleveland and its people. It is not a plan, at least not in the traditional sense. It is not a series of colored maps and designs describing an ideal future in terms of land uses, public facilities and transportation routes.
>
> Rather, it is a catalog of objectives, policies and action programs which recognizes that the urban crisis in Cleveland has little to do with land uses, zoning or urban designs and much to do with personal and municipal poverty, deteriorated housing, inadequate public transportation, and declining neighborhoods. It addresses these issues as problems to which city planners, as well as other serious public administrators, owe their time and attention ... One goal underlies the policy recommendations in this Report:

In a context of limited resources, the Cleveland City Planning Commission will give priority attention to the task of promoting a wider range of choices for those individuals and groups who have few, if any, choices.

Given the disparities in income and power between the residents of the City of Cleveland and those of the surrounding region, this goal, in part, simply reflects our responsibility and commitment to serve the people of the City.

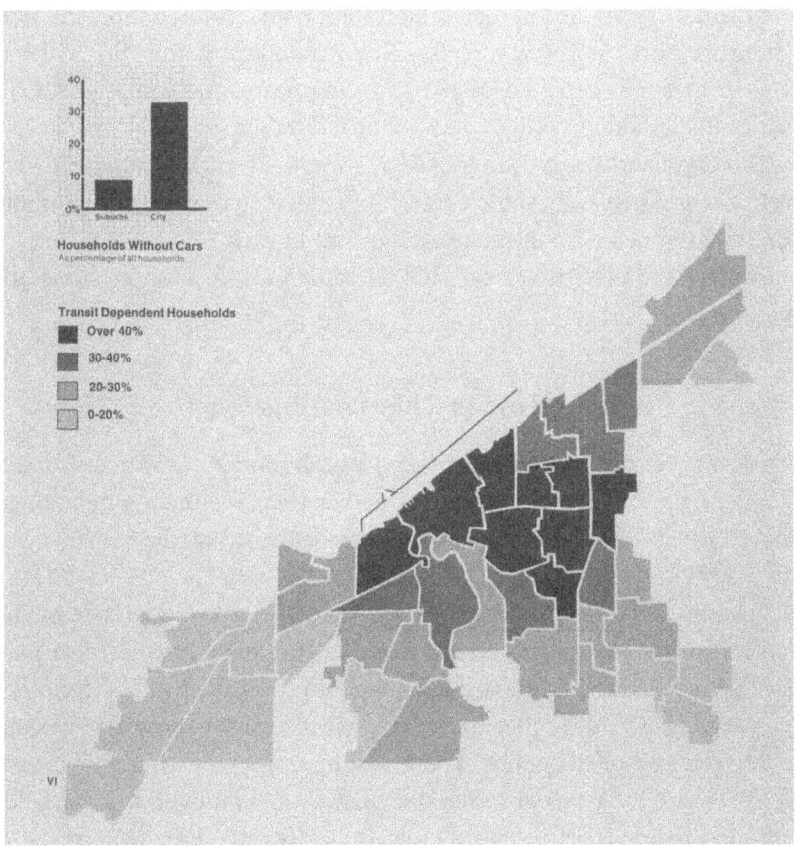

Figure 6.1 The Cleveland Policy Plan. Credit: Cleveland (Ohio). City Planning Commission, "Cleveland Policy Planning Report" (1975). *Ernie Bonner Collection*, http://archives.pdx.edu/ds/psu/14791

This may not seem like a bold statement today, but in the era right after urban renewal, the Cleveland City Planning Commission—no doubt prodded by Krumholz—deserve some credit for thinking outside the conventional planning box.

Following this groundbreaking work, planners all over the country followed Krumholz's lead. The era of the policy plan—which focused on social equity as much as buildings—would reach its peak in the next 20 years. Some might suggest that the rise of the New Urbanist movement was a response to this advocacy planning and a suggestion that it had strayed too far from the roots of urban planning.

Krumholz remained in Cleveland for ten years, through three mayoral administrations. Stokes was replaced by Republican Ralph Perk in 1971, who in turn was replaced by the left-wing firebrand Dennis Kucinich. Part of his leadership skillset was political durability.

The Cleveland Policy Plan looked at issues such as transit dependency in an era dominated by vehicle travel. After leaving Cleveland, Krumholz continued to be active in the planning community. He taught at Cornell University and also served on public boards until just before his death in 2019.

How Is This Leading?

Whatever you think of the advocacy planning model, you may wonder if it is really sort of "anti-planning" rather than leading. As mentioned above, aren't you just a conduit of information from the public as an advocacy planner?

In some ways, yes. You are not expected to be far in front of the public and leading toward a brave new world, as urban renewal leaders may have seen themselves. You are not supposed to dismiss public concerns out of hand. On the other hand, you are also not expected to simply follow the lead of the public. There will be times when the public raise concerns and look to you to develop answers. As an expert in the field, you can provide tools and techniques for addressing these concerns.

At the same time, there may be times when you use your expertise to enter into a dialogue with the public and offer a competing viewpoint. For example, some residents of a neighborhood may oppose a new apartment building due to concerns that it will gentrify their working-class neighborhood. It may be your job to explain that the gentrification may happen regardless and that the new apartments may help retain some affordability.

Leading in this way requires some compromises. You need to be open to the fact that you may not immediately have all the answers people are seeking. You may change course in the process of planning, based on what you hear and additional data you have collected. That does not make you less of a leader. Speaking up for the disadvantaged and providing them a voice in a process that is generally tilted against them—if they know it is going on at all—takes confidence. The best leaders have the confidence to bring others along for the ride.

Leading through Advocacy in the Twenty-First Century

To younger planners today, these concepts may seem almost as archaic as old-school urban renewal. However, they are very much alive and part of leading planning efforts today. You may not realize that they are because they are so ingrained into how we practice the profession today.

For example, thing about how we plan for housing today. In the urban renewal era, someone decided how many below-market affordable units were needed in a city and then planned to build them. Doing so often ignored the concerns and interests of residents, and tended to result in housing units that were not durable and subject to turnover, or even abandonment.

The followers of Jane Jacobs sometimes took a hands-off approach to housing issues. Planners should generally leave housing the way it is and let the natural processes of the city take care of it. Interestingly, in *The Death and Life of Great American Cities*, Jacobs (1992 [1961]) actually laid out a strategy for housing production. Her concept is remarkably similar to the housing voucher program in the U.S. today. Nonetheless, she did not think much of government efforts to produce housing.

Today's planners are living in a world where there are government programs, like the Low-Income Housing Tax Credit, that fund below-market affordable housing. However, neighborhoods often resist efforts to produce new housing with these programs.

If planners were simply supposed to echo the public concerns about an issue, leading planners would fight this housing production. Instead, we are often leading the charge when a proposal for such a development is made.

Why is that?

Because we know two things. One is that the data shows a need for more housing at those price points, and likely in the communities in which developers propose them. The other is that we know there are many residents that are naturally disadvantaged in the usual processes, and we take it upon ourselves to speak up for them. These residents may not be literate in planning hearings and housing finance. That doesn't mean they don't deserve a voice in this process.

So today's planning leaders, echoing the appeal of Davidoff, speak for them and advocate for things that may not be immediately popular. That doesn't mean we don't make compromises with other stakeholders—we just make sure that the playing field is levelled.

Planning was changed indelibly by the advocacy planning model. It is worth factoring into your personal leadership strategy.

Bibliography

Checkoway, Barry. 1994. "Paul Davidoff and Advocacy Planning in Retrospect," *Journal of the American Planning Association* 60:2, 140–141. DOI: 10.1080/01944369408975562.

Cleveland City Planning Commission. 1975. "Cleveland Policy Planning Report," *Ernie Bonner Collection*, http://archives.pdx.edu/ds/psu/14791.

Davidoff, Paul. 1965. "Advocacy and Pluralism in Planning," *Journal of the American Institute of Planners* 31:4, 331–338. DOI: 10.1080/01944366508978187

Jacobs, Jane. 1992 [1961]. *The Death and Life of Great American Cities*. New York: Vintage Books.

LeGates, Richard T., and Stout, Frederic. 2020. *The City Reader* (7th edn). Abingdon: Routledge.

South Burlington County NAACP v. Mount Laurel Township, 92 N.J., 158 (1983).

7

FACILITATIVE LEADERSHIP

People don't always agree. There are a variety of people involved in any planning decision and not all of them will want the same things. Even if you focus your energy on those who are traditionally not given a seat at the table, you may find that there is discord there as well. In fact, one important lesson for planners to learn about the public is that it's inaccurate to overgeneralize. Not everyone with a certain background thinks alike.

I sometimes think that the planner is really a mediator. While you do play a role in the process, a lot of planning is taking differing views and trying to come up with a balanced recommendation for how to move forward.

As many planners can appreciate, it often feels like our decisions make everyone unhappy. On the other hand, if you are working with a wide range of people, perhaps your goal isn't to make any one segment of the group too happy. I was once told that if everyone is just a little bit unhappy, that may mean you've done your job.

Is mediating the opposite of leading? Potentially. However, as practiced by a seasoned planner, mediating conflict is a unique and valuable way of leading. John Forester, a planner and professor at Cornell

University, refers to the mediation process as "facilitative leadership." In his book *Planning in the Face of Conflict*, he allows several planners to relate their experiences with mediation. However, in the introduction, he offers this perspective:

> In everyday language, these facilitative leaders have to be good listeners. They have to be sensitive to emotion and not run from it. They have to be able to pay attention without being easily distracted, either by appeals to fact or to emotion when either one turns out to be irrelevant in the case at hand. They have to be keenly alert to all the ways that disputing parties can hurt or provoke one another, not working through but escalating tensions by being dismissive or disrespectful or arrogant or overly aggressive or humiliating or racist or sexist. (Forester 2013, xv)

Like advocacy planners, the facilitative leader has to be a good listener. In this case, however, your leadership is as much about pulling the situation out of conflict as it is about coming up with the actual solution. You may end up with a compromise that you are not entirely thrilled with. On the other hand, you have turned enemies into participating parties who may end up getting along.

Like in the Advocacy Planning model, there is some question about how mediation allows room for a planner to utilize any leading skills or even perhaps to plan at all. Think about the most basic mediation situation. Two people are arguing about the price of something. Perhaps one person already sold it to the other, but didn't reveal some defect in the item. As shown below, these differing senses of value could theoretically be resolved by a mediated settlement.

In this case, it may just be simple mathematics. The mediation process comes up with a value somewhere in the middle, with perhaps some other agreements such as an offering from the seller to help fix the problem. It can be as simple as the math shown in Figure 7.1, splitting the value in half.

It often takes someone with significant skills to get angry parties to the table for such a discussion. While the likely outcome may be clear, it also may take a lot of interpersonal skills to get the parties to agree that they need to come up with a compromise. In the end, a skillful mediator with a little buy-in from participants will come up with an agreed path forward. In this example, it was as simple as splitting the difference.

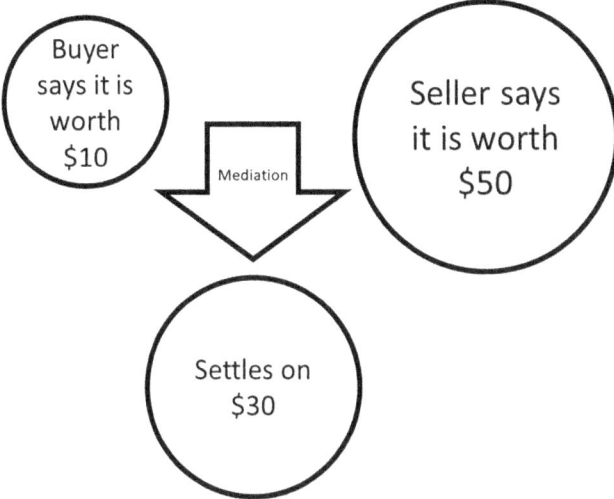

Figure 7.1 How a simple mediation over the price of an item might work. Credit: Author.

Mediation can be very useful in land use disputes as well. Someone wants to build a relatively tall building near a subdivision, and the residents are concerned about the impacts that this may have on their quality of life. Issues, both real and imagined, drive the subdivision residents to oppose the project. They get involved in the review process and use every tool imaginable to hold up the construction of the building.

At the same time, the developer of the building may have not done the best job in the world reaching out to neighbors ahead of time. She's pressed for time and her budget is tight. She thinks she has the zoning she needs to get the building in the ground and goes to the Planning Board for what she thinks is a routine approval.

Instead, she runs into two hours of testimony from the neighbors and their lawyers about how bad the project will be for their quality of life. They refer to specific standards in the zoning ordinance that they say are being violated.

They may be being unreasonable, but they may also have a point. The Planning Board decides to postpone a vote and asks both parties to meet with a mediator to settle the issues.

Already, this situation is much more complex than averaging $10 and $50. A skilled mediator will have to work with both parties to determine if mediation is even likely to help. If it is, the mediator then has to help the parties come up with an agreed-upon set of facts. For example, how tall is the building? How will you look at shadow impacts? How will the parties evaluate traffic impacts—just at rush hour, or all day long, or both?

The mediator then has to enter into a discussion about what is and is not up for discussion. Finally, the mediator will have to do the hard work of trying to get both parties to agree to a path forward. This may involve developing a building that is less tall. It may also involve how the building is designed, or where it sends its stormwater, or how traffic circulation works. It's unlikely to result in an agreement to build something half as tall as the original proposal, although that is possible.

This scenario will no doubt require an experienced and skillful mediator. This is a rare and coveted talent. It will also probably require a mediator with some experience in land use and planning processes. An important part of resolving this dispute is an understanding of what the Planning Board can ask of the developer. Does she simply have the right to build the building? Or does the Board have to waive some requirements or give some discretionary approvals?

So, a mediator with planning experience would be helpful in this situation. However, is this a satisfying role for a planner—especially a planner who is looking to take the lead on positive change? How can you institute change when your primary goal is to come to a solution that works for two or more outside parties?

In some ways this dilemma resembles that of the advocate planner in Chapter 6. In that case, the question was whether there is a role for planning leaders in speaking up for those who are unable to speak for themselves. In this case, the question is whether there is a role for planning leaders when you are trying to resolve conflict between interested parties.

> **WHAT IS MEDIATION ANYWAY?**
>
> The concept of mediation gets a great deal of attention in planning practice. It's important to take a quick step back and determine what we mean by mediation.

Mediation is a concept that is widely used in the legal profession, so it's helpful to look at how lawyers define it. The American Bar Association says that mediation is:

> [A] private process where a neutral third person called a mediator helps the parties discuss and try to resolve the dispute. The parties have the opportunity to describe the issues, discuss their interests, understandings, and feelings; provide each other with information and explore ideas for the resolution of the dispute. While courts can mandate that certain cases go to mediation, the process remains "voluntary" in that the parties are not required to come to agreement. The mediator does not have the power to make a decision on behalf of the parties, but can help the parties find a resolution that is mutually acceptable. The only people who can resolve the dispute in mediation are the parties themselves. There are a number of different ways that a mediation can proceed. Most mediations start with the parties together in a joint session. The mediator will describe how the process works, will explain the mediator's role and will help establish ground rules and an agenda for the session. Generally, parties then make opening statements. Some mediators conduct the entire process in a joint session. However, other mediators will move to separate sessions, shuttling back and forth between the parties. If the parties reach an agreement, the mediator may help reduce the agreement to a written contract, which may be enforceable in court.

Key to the idea of mediation is that it is voluntary. Also key to the idea is that each party has a chance to express their views. While the American Bar Association doesn't highlight this idea, it's also important to try to establish a generally accepted set of facts. If both parties can't agree on a basic truth (i.e. how tall a building is), there will be a challenge in terms of coming to agreement.

Planners have tweaked the definition a bit at times. As discussed in this chapter, a planner also serving as a mediator may be serving two roles—and there may be challenges associated with doing so.

Leading through Mediation

Planners have thought about this issue. John Forester spent a lot of time thinking about the role of how planners can implement good planning through mediation. "In the face of local land-use conflicts," he asked, "how can planners mediate between conflicting parties and at the same time negotiate as interested parties themselves?" (Forester 1989, 82).

The idea that you could be both a mediator and one of the mediating parties was controversial among some mediators. If you have a stake in the outcome, how can you mediate properly? Forester suggests six strategies for planners, each of which has different implications for these dual roles (adapted from Forester 1989, 88–96):

1. *Planner as regulator.* This is an almost judicial role, in which the planner establishes the facts and clarifies how to examine an issue. In the end, however, this is a fairly hands-off approach with less direct input.
2. *Pre-mediate and negotiate.* Somewhat similar to the advocacy planner role, in this case the planner speaks up for other stakeholders who are not in the room. In doing so, the hope is that they may be able to avoid mediation being necessary after the fact.
3. *The planner as resource.* In this case, the planner offers advice to parties on how to keep their discussions moving, but, unlike the pre-mediation role above, the planner is not generally present during these discussions. A common strategy used under this model is when a planner recommends to a developer to meet with the neighborhood. They may not attend that meeting, but may recommend it as part of good practice.
4. *Shuttle diplomacy.* In this model, the planner is most active as a mediator, but in private settings. They go from party to party and back, proposing solutions that may help satisfy the other party's concerns. However, there is still not much of a role for their professional opinions.
5. *Active and interested mediation.* In this case, the planner is acting most like a mediator, with one difference. As a member of the city staff or in some other similar institutional role in the community, they

hope to utilize their investment in the community to build goodwill on both sides. They are not an outside party coming in to settle things, but a professional with a direct stake in the outcome, if not an ability to advance their own agenda.

6. *Split the job—you Mediate, I'll negotiate.* In this model, a planner might bring in another party, such as a Planning Board member, to play the role of mediator and allow the planner to play the role of one of the interested parties. This is the most comfortable role for a planner who has strong feelings about the issues at hand, as they will not have to play two different roles.

ASSESSING MEDIATION POTENTIAL: ASSEMBLY SQUARE

Early in my career, I was the planner for a major redevelopment project in Somerville, Massachusetts. The Assembly Square urban renewal area was originally railroad yards and a Ford manufacturing plant. In the late 1970s the closed plant was redeveloped into a shopping mall as part of an urban renewal plan that does not appear to have been entirely free from political influence. The mall lasted for 20 years or so, and then the site was clearly declining and in need of a new planning effort.

Unlike in many circumstances, this time there were many residents who wanted to see a dense, mixed-use development on the site. The city where I worked was interested in fast redevelopment. In this case, that likely meant big box retail. A group of residents with experience and interest in urban design, public finance, and planning formed a group called the "Mystic View Site Task Force" (later simply the "Mystic View Task Force") to look at redevelopment of the site. They concluded that the best plan was what they called "30/30/30." This plan involved 30 acres of new open space, 30 million square feet of development, and $30 million a year in tax revenue for the City.

While City staff were supportive of these concepts, we also felt the pressure from political leaders to see a fast redevelopment of the site. Somerville has a two-year mayoral term, leading to pressure for quick actions. Of all the staff in City Hall, I was the one most in the middle— I was the liaison to the Mystic View Task Force!

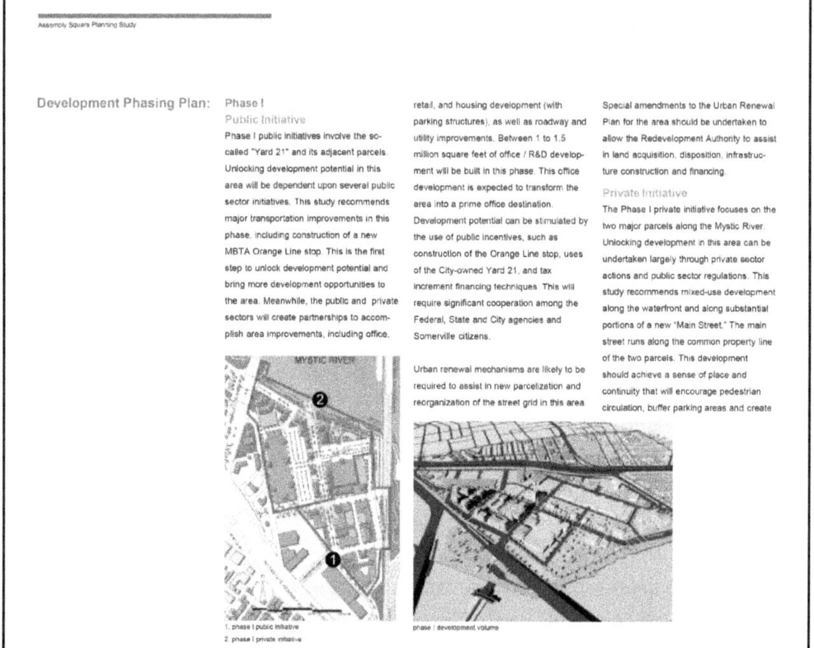

Assembly Square Planning Study

Development Phasing Plan: Phase I

Public Initiative

Phase I public initiatives involve the so-called "Yard 21" and its adjacent parcels. Unlocking development potential in this area will be dependent upon several public sector initiatives. This study recommends major transportation improvements in this phase, including construction of a new MBTA Orange Line stop. This is the first step to unlock development potential and bring more development opportunities to the area. Meanwhile, the public and private sectors will create partnerships to accomplish area improvements, including office, retail, and housing development (with parking structures), as well as roadway and utility improvements. Between 1 to 1.5 million square feet of office / R&D development will be built in this phase. This office development is expected to transform the area into a prime office destination. Development potential can be stimulated by the use of public incentives, such as construction of the Orange Line stop, uses of the City-owned Yard 21, and tax increment financing techniques. This will require significant cooperation among the Federal, State and City agencies and Somerville citizens.

Urban renewal mechanisms are likely to be required to assist in new parcelization and reorganization of the street grid in this area. Special amendments to the Urban Renewal Plan for the area should be undertaken to allow the Redevelopment Authority to assist in land acquisition, disposition, infrastructure construction and financing.

Private Initiative

The Phase I private initiative focuses on the two major parcels along the Mystic River. Unlocking development in this area can be undertaken largely through private sector actions and public sector regulations. This study recommends mixed-use development along the waterfront and along substantial portions of a new "Main Street." The main street runs along the common property line of the two parcels. This development should achieve a sense of place and continuity that will encourage pedestrian circulation, buffer parking areas and create

1. phase I public initiative
2. phase I private initiative

phase I development volume

Figure 7.2 Excerpt from the City of Somerville's Assembly Square Planning Study (2000). Credit: City of Somerville, Massachusetts.

We were able to complete a planning study of the area, but the result was a phased approach that relied on big box retail in the early phases and postponed the mixed-use portions of development until later. That was not satisfactory to active residents.

To cut a long story very short, this situation eventually escalated to the point of lawsuits. The state, which had an interest in successful redevelopment of the site, stepped in and sought to find a solution to the conflict. They hired the Consensus Building Institute to conduct a mediation assessment, looking at whether mediation was a possible approach to resolving the situation.

City staff were wary—in part because the state leaders working on this situation included a member of the Mystic View Task Force. In addition, we felt there was little wiggle room, given our political leadership. However, we wanted to try.

Mediation assessment included interviews with stakeholders and a long roundtable discussion at a local university. In the end, there did

> not seem to be a high probability that mediation would resolve the issue. The litigation route would have to play itself out.
>
> A few years later, with a new Mayor and changes in other players, mediation ended up playing a major role in resolving development issues in Assembly Square. The result is a major mixed-use redevelopment—with some large retail as well. In the long run, mediation did what lawsuits could not.

Mediation Is Leading: A Stronger View on This Link

Forester suggests that there are ways to mediate planning disputes without giving up a voice in the process. He even suggests it's possible to lead an initiative with a strong mediating role. That is inspiring to planners who often see their role as playing the traffic cop in a process rather than driving in the front of the parade.

There is also a line of thinking that pushes the link between mediation and leading even further. Lawrence Susskind, a planning professor at the Massachusetts Institute of Technology, has spent his career not just teaching and researching, but also actively leading mediation processes. When it comes to mediation and leadership, he sees more than a possible détente—he sees a strong partnership.

Forester describes Susskind well:

> No one has done more than Larry Susskind to demonstrate the promise of mediation, facilitative leadership, and consensus building for governance and planning in the face of conflict. For more than 40 years Susskind has worked not only with local organizations to resolve housing, land-use, and transportation disputes, but with international organizations to address global environmental issues—more recently, for example, challenges of water diplomacy.
>
> Susskind fits no stereotype of a typical university professor. Teaching in the Massachusetts Institute of Technology's Department of Urban Studies and Planning, he has complemented his steady stream of

publications with an even more active professional life as a mediator, trainer, and policy advisor, in the U.S. and abroad. In any given year, Susskind has been in the middle of a halfdozen multiparty, multi-issue disputes involving, for example, the siting of hazardous waste facilities, the design of controversial regional public housing plans, the creation of city-suburb costsharing schemes to ensure regional water quality, or the crafting of toxic waste cleanup strategies involving industry, government, and community members.

Susskind's vision of public dispute mediation and his successful practice make him a widely respected, if at times controversial figure in the dispute resolution community. Both his vision and practice challenged the popular wisdom of the field that regards "neutrality" as sacred. Many mediators might have concerned themselves with process alone, leaving the substance of agreements to the parties themselves. The demands of neutrality, according to many public dispute mediators, prevent them from focusing on power imbalances among negotiating parties. Other mediators working in the public eye wonder if mediation can be a viable strategy when participants number 30 or more, the process is highly political, and parties vary enormously in their expertise, resources, and political experience.

Susskind rejects mediator claims to pure neutrality. He suggests, instead, a stricter notion of nonpartisanship and the provocative idea of activist mediation. He has argued that mediators must address power imbalances among the parties to public disputes by, for example, providing premediation negotiation training to all parties.

Susskind's early statements to the planning profession remain accessible, clearly argued, and practically relevant, even as they gave way to his more monumental *Consensus Building Handbook* and smaller guides to practice (for example, *Breaking Robert's Rules*), with other volumes documenting emerging ideas and practices published in between and since. Susskind's influence has been extensive, and it has contributed as well to the broader Program on Negotiation at Harvard that he has shaped since its earliest days. (Forester 2013, 261–262)

Susskind's Consensus Building Institute has been contributing to leading planning efforts in the Boston region and far beyond for many years. The Institute conducts assessments as to whether mediation is worth the effort, as well as mediation services for planning clients and others. The planner is seen as an interested party, and therefore is not burdened with the effort of providing mediation services as well as advancing a viewpoint. Like Forester's "Split the Job" concept, this frees the mediators to mediate and the planner to speak up for best practices. Susskind's idea of "activist mediation" allows you to lead and also resolve conflicts.

Susskind's view is that the old-fashioned idea of the leader—as in the model of a military leader or strong Chief Executive Officer—is outdated. Instead, the complex challenges of the current world require a leadership model that involves the facilitation and distribution of responsibilities. This model, while applicable in a variety of settings, would be particularly relevant in the world of planning.

MEDIATION AS A MESSAGE TO BE REASONABLE: THE SAINT AIDAN

Figure 7.3 Saint Aidan's during construction. Credit: Tom Kelly under a Creative Commons 2.0 License, https://creativecommons.org/licenses/by-sa/2.0/legalcode

Sometimes mediation may not work, but helps resolve an issue anyway.

My first job leading an entire planning office was in the town of Brookline, Massachusetts. This town, larger than many cities, retained many elements of small-town government, including a Town Meeting. On the other hand, it has many areas denser than most large cities. By some calculations—a little overstated but not entirely off-base—parts of Brookline have more people living in every square mile than Bangkok, Thailand.

Density is a good thing for sustainability and walkability. It can also cause planning conflicts. One of the major projects I worked on was an adaptive reuse of a former church site into mixed-income housing.

This wasn't just any church. Saint Aidan's was the boyhood parish of John F. Kennedy's family, who lived down the street. He was baptized there. So, when the church closed in the late 1990s, it wasn't that surprising that there would be a lot of interest in the future of the site. Add to that a relatively wealthy community and a form of government that works by almost unanimous consent, and the reuse of the site was likely to be a big news item for years.

A non-profit developer proposed demolishing the church and parish house, and building almost 200 units of low-income housing. While the need for the housing was apparent, the loss of the church and the scale of the project caused significant resistance. Working with town planners and leaders, the developer ended up with a revised proposal that would reuse the church building as high-end condominiums and produce a much smaller number of low-income units in a mid-rise building.

However, even that proposal was not acceptable to neighbors. As planning staff, we tried a variety of Forester's approaches. We did "shuttle diplomacy." We played it straight as a resource or as a regulator. Nothing seemed to work.

When one last lawsuit was filed, one step in the process was attempted mediation with a third party. In this case, as with Assembly Square, town planners as well as other leaders were parties in the dispute. That again freed us up to play an active role, as well as to attempt to bring the two sides to come to an agreement. We honestly felt the developer had made every concession she could in this project and that the neighbors were being unreasonable. On the other hand, we wanted a good resolution to the situation. Mediation helped frame the discussion.

While the mediation did not work in this case, it may have helped the neighbors understand how unreasonable their demands were. The project had already been significantly scaled back, and open space and the church were being preserved.

Bibliography

American Bar Association. "Mediation." See https://www.americanbar.org/groups/dispute_resolution/resources/DisputeResolutionProcesses/mediation.

Forester, John. 1989. *Planning in the Face of Power.* Berkeley, CA: University of California Press.

Forester, John. 2013. *Planning in the Face of Conflict.* Chicago, IL: Planners Press.

8

STRATEGIC PLANNING AND LEADERSHIP

If you are a good manager of a planning office—as many of you no doubt are—you are good at keeping things moving along. Projects and programs occur in predictable patterns. You know when you need to get packets of reports out to the Board and you know when your reporting deadlines are for grants. You apply for funds from state and private sources, and often get the money!

Running an office can feel like being on a track. You go around the track and do your best. Then you go around again. This isn't a bad thing. Keeping the silent machines of government running smoothly is harder than it seems.

However, it doesn't really qualify as leading. Leadership means taking your planning efforts and taking them to the next level. You may have a good system for producing staff reports, but you likely inherited this from former planners. You probably don't change it that much. So while it does what it needs to do, maybe it's not doing what it could do.

Think of your work as a mechanical system, such as an assembly line that makes cars. You can keep making cars the way you have always done. You know how to do that. Your office does a good job of assembling cars.

However, it takes hours to make each car because people are operating the assembly line in ways that are not always cost-effective.

You could pick up a copy of *The Principles of Scientific Management* and figure out ways to make your assembly line operate more efficiently. Maybe parts can be stored closer to where they are needed. Maybe you can put parts together on a sideline before putting them on the car. These changes would help.

However, there's a bigger problem. Your cars are fine, but you're not sure they are the best cars you could assemble. All your cars are the same and you know your market is looking for different kinds of cars. You may even want to build scooters and bikes.

Figuring out what you should make—in addition to how to make them efficiently—is strategic planning. Understanding and implementing strategic planning is an important leadership skill. This chapter provides a review of what strategic planning is, how to start with a strategic planning effort, and why it is important to leading.

This is not a book about strategic planning in the public sector. Fortunately, there is already a good book on this subject. John Bryson, a planning professor at the Humphrey School of Public Affairs at the University of Minnesota, is an expert on this subject. His book, *Strategic Planning for Public and Nonprofit Organizations: A Guide to Strengthening and Sustaining Organizational Achievement* (Bryson 2017), has lots of good ideas on this subject. This chapter summarizes some of its key concepts, with a little of my editorializing on the side!

While strategic planning can be intimidating, time-consuming, and difficult to keep on track, it's important for organizations. It also doesn't need to be done perfectly. If you don't have time to do everything required, it's fine to do what you can. The important thing about thinking strategically is to take some time to do so.

Benefits of Strategic Planning

According to Bryson, strategic planning has many benefits for public agencies:

1. It promotes strategic acts for your organization as well as learning. Your organization can have a "strategic conversation" and think about how it should achieve its goals in the context of a changing environment.

2. It improves your decision-making process by focusing attention on the crucial issues and challenges your organization faces.
3. It makes your organization more effective, responsive, resilient, and sustainable by clarifying major issues facing your organization, and helps you deal with them wisely.
4. It enhances your organizational legitimacy by bringing stakeholders into the process. Public agencies earn the right to exist by explaining how they create public value at reasonable costs, and strategic planning helps you to do so.
5. It enhances the effectiveness of what you do by looking at other organizations and figuring out who does what well. Sometimes things you work on may be moved to other places, and sometimes things that others are doing will be moved into your organization.
6. It directly benefits your staff by building their confidence and morale, and reducing their anxiety. Staff play an important part of the process of strategic planning (Bryson 2017, 14–16).

This may read a little bit like an ad pitch for a new product, but it's really an appeal to step back from your day-to-day activities and struggles. Bring people who may have opinions and ideas to the table. Question the usual assumptions about what you need to do. Start with what you want to get done, not how you do it.

"The Paradox of Strategic Planning"

Unfortunately, the organizations that would most benefit from strategic planning are the ones that are least likely to do so. Bryson calls this "the paradox of strategic planning" (Bryson 2017, 17). While some of these organizations are simply running on autopilot, some of them have extremely talented leaders. The argument is that you don't need to engage in a process when you have such a clear vision of what needs to change and how to change it.

Talented leaders who have great ideas sometimes forget a couple of key facts:

- They are not always right!
- Even when they are right, they can get a lot more done with their ideas when they enjoy strong support.

There are some rare moments for leaders to push their organization in a certain direction. Public agencies in particular have a lot of internal resistance to organizational change. People are comfortable doing things a certain way, both because it's easy and also because it generally works. There's no incentive to change if things are working. There is also risk associated with change and there is the concern that if changes don't work, you will be blamed for this.

In these cases, as a leader, you need to push. However, instead of pushing a predetermined path of change, you should push your organization to engage in a strategic planning process. While you may have some good ideas about where that process will take you, don't announce them ahead of time. If they are good ideas, they will emerge from the process. When they do, they will have the legitimacy of a communal process.

The other challenge for strategic planning is from above. While we talked in Chapter 4 about how to lead your bosses, in this case, you need to simply get them to let you plan broadly. Your boss needs to understand there is risk associated with changing your organization, but there are also likely to be benefits. At the very least, you will discover that you have been doing things the right way all along.

Having the courage to enter into a process like strategic planning is leadership. Bryson is careful to note that leadership is key to a successful process:

> Furthermore, strategic planning is not a substitute for leadership broadly conceived. In my experience, there is simply *no* substitute for leadership when it comes to engaging in strategic planning effectively. At least some key decision makers and process champions must be committed to it; otherwise, any attempts to use strategic planning are bound to fail. (Bryson 2017, 18)

You will also need to keep leading the process. It's one thing to launch an inclusive, broad process for looking strategically at your organization and goals; it's quite another thing to make sure it stays on track without being seen as putting your thumb on the scales.

The Strategic Planning Process

There is not enough space in this book to explain the strategic planning process in detail. There are other good books that do that. However, it's worth giving an overview of the process. Generally, it has nine steps:

1. First, initiate the process and agree on what it will (and won't) be. This is one of the places where leadership is most important. If you are going to look at just your development review process, make sure the process is tailored for that task. If it strays into other territory—say, your neighborhood planning process—it will be important for you to bring the process back on track.
2. Identify your organizational mandates. What is your organization created to do? Who created it?
3. Clarify your organization's mission and values. What perspective does it bring to accomplishing the mandate and how does that affect how it meets it?
4. Assess internal and external environments. While this can be done in many ways, the most common is the "SWOT" analysis, which looks at your organizational Strengths, Weaknesses, Opportunities, and Threats (see "Doing a SWOT Analysis" below).
5. Once you have identified these environmental factors, identify the key strategic issues facing your organization. This may be a subset of the SWOT list or all of them.
6. Develop strategies to address those key issues.
7. Review these strategies and adopt them as a strategic plan.
8. Establish an effective organizational vision that is based on the plan.
9. Reassess the strategies and the process, and revisit as needed! (Bryson 2017, 38)

DOING A SWOT ANALYSIS

Every organization and place has a range of good and bad things to consider when thinking about change. A common way to explore these assets is through a "SWOT" analysis that looks at the Strengths, Weaknesses, Opportunities, and Threats facing that organization or

STRATEGIC PLANNING AND LEADERSHIP 131

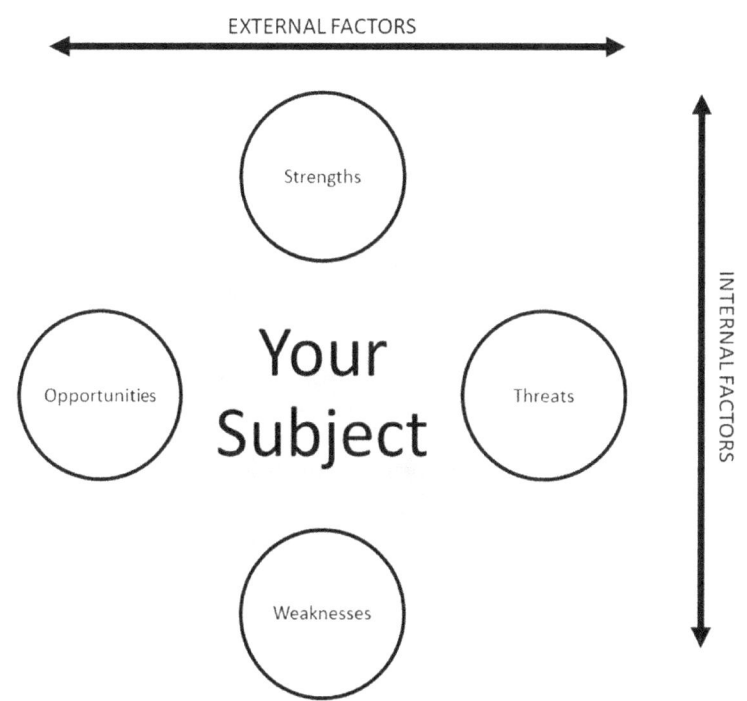

Figure 8.1 Mapping out a SWOT analysis. Credit: Author.

place. While there are many forms of the SWOT analysis, they are all generally variations on the same theme.

The basic process—which can be done by laypersons with little expertise other than some basic crowd management skills and a good pen and a large pad—is interactive. The activity leader posts a large piece of paper on the wall (or four—one for each of the four elements). The audience is encouraged to volunteer ideas that they have regarding the organization or place being studied. The facilitator places the ideas into one (or more) of the four categories and helps build a map of sorts as to what challenges and potential to think about in changing that organization or place:

- Strengths are existing, positive internal attributes.
- Weaknesses are existing, negative internal attributes.

> - Opportunities are external, positive factors from which the organization or place might benefit.
> - Threats are external, negative factors that might challenge the organization or place.
>
> While mapping these four concepts out may not answer the question of what to do about them, it helps structure your thinking and plan for future action.

Strategic Planning versus Leadership

While strategic planning is important, it is not a substitute for leadership. However, it takes leadership to succeed.

It takes "leadership," not just a "leader." One of the key lessons for planning leaders from the strategic planning model is that leadership is far larger than an individual person. Leadership may not even be formal "Executive Directors" or CEOs. Bryson describes the leaders that make up leadership as:

> [P]eople who use both formal and informal authority, as well as other assets, to help achieve worthy outcomes and contribute to societal well-being. (Bryson 2017, 354)

This idea that the true leaders may not just be the "boss" is not limited to strategic planning. However, in a strategic planning process, the group of leaders may be even more fluid. These leaders that make up "leadership" may not even be the same people over time:

> Indeed, the same people will be leaders and followers at different times over the course of a strategy change cycle. (Bryson 2017, 354)

Those who have an opportunity to lead may find that opportunity fleeting and should use it while they can.

The Role of Leadership in Strategic Planning

If we aren't entirely sure who the leaders are in strategic planning, maybe we can at least figure out what they are supposed to do. However, this isn't a simple job.

Strategic planning leaders need to have a broad set of skills and the wisdom that comes with understanding an organization and its context well. They need to keep a process going that people may not have time for, and probably don't have a lot of interest in. At the same time, they need to get their regular jobs done.

Generally, here are some things that leadership should do to keep a strategic planning process effective:

- Understand the context (but don't get captured by past history).
- Understand the people involved (including yourself) and be open to feedback.
- Sponsor the process. Commit the resources necessary and be willing to use authority to keep it going.
- Champion the process (keep it on people's agendas).
- Facilitate the process (be enthusiastic and help get it unstuck when necessary).
- Foster collective leadership (don't do it all on your own—rely on teams).
- Use dialogue and deliberation to create a meaningful process (including who does what).
- Make and implement policy decisions (avoid "bureaucratic imprisonment").
- Be a boss (enforce rules, settle disputes, and manage conflicts).
- Put it all together and be prepared that it may need to be done again soon (adapted from Bryson 2017, 354)!

Completing an effective strategic planning process takes a lot of hands-on work from leaders, starting with who the leaders are and then seeing it through. It's worth making sure your organization is ready for it and what the indicators of success are.

Sometimes the process itself is the success. On the other hand, it's particularly rewarding when the process identifies things that should change and you make those changes—and then your organization becomes better! That's leadership.

Strategic Planning for the Busy Planning Leader

If this all seems intimidating to you, you're not alone. Many planners are overwhelmed by the idea of conducting a strategic planning exercise for their office. With the Mayor calling, angry neighbors, and a high-maintenance board to staff (or two), making time for strategic planning can be tough. If a strategic planning process requires your full attention, maybe you just shouldn't bother.

This concern is understandable. On the other hand, if you have problems with your current processes and feel your organization veers from crisis to crisis, you won't fix that situation without some form of strategic planning.

Is there an option that allows you to make some progress on thinking strategically even if can't commit to a full-blown process? Fortunately, there are several:

- *Focus on a specific subject.* If you don't have time to lead a formal strategic planning process or if you are just exploring your options, you can start with a smaller subject. Pick a current problem you need to figure out—such as an upset neighborhood or problems with retaining downtown businesses—and focus a shorter process on that problem.
- *Start with a mission statement.* One way to get people in your office to start thinking strategically is to figure out your organization's mission—not just "what do we do every week?" but "why do we do it?" This is a simple process that can be done through email much of the time. You can work through several iterations of a mission statement until you figure out what makes sense. The best part is that there is nothing binding about this process. It's simply a chance to engage your team in some strategic thinking—and to show some leadership by pushing them to resolve complex and conflicting goals that planners face.

- *Start with a SWOT analysis.* If you have limited time, you can get your team together to complete an analysis of your organization's strengths and weaknesses, and external opportunities and threats. Even completing this initial phase gives you (and everyone in your office) a sense of where you fit in.
- *Do something interactive with your team.* In some ways, the process is the result when you are thinking strategically. If you don't have the time to even do one of these limited strategic processes, or you have a better idea, just get everyone together to talk about your organization. It can be an open conversation or structured around looking at your budget or deliverables. Just taking the time to explore larger issues will have some strategic benefit.

Doing something to think about the direction of your organization differentiates leaders from managers. It's not enough to simply say you are busy. You need to bring your team along on a journey to explore what they should be doing to accomplish their organizational goals. That may start with something as simple as figuring out what those goals are!

Does Strategic Planning Work in a Public Planning Office?

Strategic planning originated as a tool for businesses to figure out their next moves. To some, this raises the question of whether it can be effectively used in a public sector office.

The concept of bringing best practices to the public sector from the private sector is not new. Ideas like zero-based budgeting and even professional human resource management have been brought over to government offices, with some success. However, it's fair to ask the question of how much of the tool is really useful in a different context.

In a planning office, there are similar questions about strategic planning. How much control do you really have over your workplan? You can't stop applicants from submitting their projects for review. You also can't control where all the funding comes from. If you want to build below-market affordable housing, for example, you may have to build the kinds for which federal grants exist.

As a hopeful leader in planning, it may be challenging to think about the limits to your control. On the other hand, it shouldn't be a big surprise.

John Forester raises the issue succinctly in his book *Planning in the Face of Power*:

> Notice that planners who seek to meet public needs face even greater challenges than their more romanticized private-sector counterparts, the corporate "strategic" planners. For publicly oriented planners need to worry not only about waste but also about social justice; they need to worry not only about efficiency but also about decent outcomes; they need to worry not only about satisfied customers but also about the food, housing and jobs the perfect market promises and the actual market fails to provide. Compared to the job that public-sector planners have, the planners with private-sector clients has it easy. (Forester 1989, 4)

In private businesses, there are fairly clear lines of authority and decision making is centralized. In government, even in cities with strong mayors, there are often several power centers, which may not agree about strategic priorities. Even if you bring them all into a process, you may not find a clear answer.

Paul Nutt and Robert Backoff have proposed that the strategic planning concept does work in a public sector setting. They do ask for a rebranding and revision of the concept into a "strategic management" framework:

> Our approach calls for the strategic management process to be carried out by a strategic management group, hereafter termed the SMG, composed of five to 15 key members of the organization. Typically, the chief executive officer, the senior staff, and up to three levels of management responsibility are involved. It is not unusual for representatives of oversight boards or strong stakeholder groups to participate. In the mental health center case, the 14 participants all came from within the center and included its director. Outside stakeholders were involved in legitimizing the process at the beginning and became involved again during the formulation and implementation

of strategies. Outside consultants helped establish the strategic management process by holding seven four-hour meetings with the SMG. During this start-up phase, an SMG engages in a series of activities to launch the strategic management process and develop the task force as a strategic management team.

The strategic management group moves through a process that has six stages. Individual stages depict the organization's historical context in terms of its environmental trends, its overall direction, and its normative ideals; assess the immediate situation it faces in terms of current strengths and weaknesses and future opportunities and threats; develop an agenda of current strategic issues to be managed; design strategic options for managing priority issues; assess the options in terms of stakeholders affected and resources required; and implement high-priority strategies by mobilizing resources and managing stakeholders. Once the process is under way for at least one issue and one strategy to manage the issue, the stages of the process may be repeated in whole or in part. (Nutt and Backoff 1987, 45)

Public sector management and leadership is a little different—however, not so different. With some modifications, this private sector tool can be adapted to promote public leadership.

This brings to mind the quintessential issue many public sector planners have had to cope with—customer service. Every planning office I have ever worked in was told by political leaders to improve our customer service. This was not an unreasonable request—in fact, when I started at these offices, I often told staff the same thing. The challenge is that, unlike a private business, many "customers" are not voluntarily in our office. In a store, you can assume that most customers choose to come in to buy something they want. Similarly, in a private service provider's office, customers have choices of where to seek dental care or a doctor. In the end, there is a somewhat voluntary relationship with customers.

In public offices, people coming in for funding or to get their project approved are not really customers in the same way. They deserve to be treated respectfully and honestly, but sometimes the correct answer to an applicant is "no." How do we handle the fact that the customer is not always right? How can we plan strategically when our client base and funding is not related in the same way as in a coffee shop?

An interesting counterpoint to the idea that strategic planning is difficult to implement in the public sector was raised by Jerome Kaufman and Harvey Jacobs in 1987. Maybe we have it all backward! Maybe public sector planning, as practiced since the end of urban renewal, is already doing all the important parts of strategic planning! In other words, the private sector is just borrowing an idea from us:

> We conclude that most of the ideas subsumed in this approach have been a part of planning education for decades and that most practitioners trained as planners view the approach as "old wine in new bottles." Nevertheless, we argue that planners should view the new popularity of corporate-style strategic planning as an opportunity to revive interest in planning ... Whether or not the corporate strategic planning approach to planning in the public sector will prove to have been another passing fad remains to be seen. But there is no doubt that it is the center of a lot of attention nowadays. (Kaufman and Jacobs 1987, 23)

Even they end up noting there may be some things to learn from the strategic planning tools for a public office:

> Although in agreement that the two planning approaches are not fundamentally different, both the supporters and the skeptics of corporate strategic planning cited differences in emphasis between the two approaches. Both groups seemed to agree that the strategic planning approach tended to be shorter-range in focus and targeted on more realistic and feasible proposals. In addition, they were in agreement that strategic planning efforts at the local level emphasized marketing of communities attractively, packaging action proposals in ways designed to excite the public and policymakers, and highlighting the community's competitive advantages—all ideas consistent with the private-sector origins of the model. Differences of opinion did surface, however, between the supporters and the skeptics. Whereas supporters tended to assess strategic planning efforts as more analytically rigorous, as involving a broader cross section of

the community in planning, and as achieving more implementation success, skeptics—as befitted their label—disagreed with those contentions. (Kaufman and Jacobs 1987, 30)

In the end, it may be helpful to realize that private sector leaders may not have as much power as you think. In a publicly held company, they still have a Board of Directors to report to. Even internally, many business leaders are well-advised to understand the limits of their power to change course without some buy-in. So, while there are definitely some differences, they don't outweigh the benefits of thinking strategically to lead a planning organization.

Bibliography

Bryson, John. 2017. *Strategic Planning for Public and Nonprofit Organizations: A Guide to Strengthening and Sustaining Organizational Achievement* (5th edn). Hoboken, NJ: John Wiley and Sons.

Forester, John. 1989. *Planning in the Face of Power*. Berkeley, CA: University of California Press.

Kaufman, Jerome L. and Jacobs, Harvey M. 1987. "A Public Planning Perspective on Strategic Planning," *Journal of the American Planning Association*, 53:1, 23. DOI: 10.1080/01944368708976632.

Nutt, Paul C. and Backoff, Robert W. 1987. "A Strategic Management Process for Public and Third-Sector Organizations," *Journal of the American Planning Association*, 53:1, 45. DOI: 10.1080/01944368708976634.

Taylor, Frederick Winslow. 1911. *The Principles of Scientific Management*. New York: Harper & Brothers.

9

FIVE STEPS TO LEADERSHIP

Why do you want to be a planner?

This is one of my favorite job interview questions. It is also one of the best things that graduate school advisors and professors can ask their students. Unfortunately, it's a rare interview where this question is asked. Inevitably it must come up over the course of two years of graduate school, but it doesn't get the respect it deserves.

Some of the most common answers include:

- "I want to make the world a better place."
- "I want to build sustainable places."
- "I want to reduce global warming and environmental degradation."
- "I love cities and want to work on them."
- "I want to protect open space and farmland."
- "I want to develop multimodal transportation systems."

These are all very good goals—and I am sure there are others that I am have missed. The answer that rarely comes up is "I want to be a leader."

Most people do not enter urban planning to become leaders. Those who naturally desire leadership more often go into politics, get an MBA, or pursue some other path more directly related to leading. However, leading is an essential part of accomplishing all of the great planning goals that good students and employees pursue.

Planners without leadership skills often struggle to do good planning. That's because leadership is an important means to their ultimate ends. However, more often planners naturally shun leadership roles, feeling that political leaders are too busy playing politics and that management leaders don't care about lofty goals. Whatever their initial feelings about leading, planners who dismiss leadership are less effective as planners.

The Power Structure versus the Leadership Structure

Planners are natural functionalists. The idea that there are systems, and that they explain how the world works, is reinforced in most planning disciplines. Transportation planners have the four-step travel demand model. Land-use planners conduct population projections by developing spreadsheets that extrapolate births, deaths, and migrations to predict the future. Statistical analysts look at multivariate regressions and theorize that every additional year of education translates into an additional $10,000 in income (plus or minus $5,000, of course!)

So, when planners enter a work environment, they look at the organizational chart. The new planner in Yellowstone, Northwest Territories (an interesting place to do planning, as an aside) might find this chart awaiting them and feel that they understand the organization.

"I am a Planner 1 in the Planning and Lands Division. Therefore, I report to the head of that division, who reports to the head of the Planning and Development Department, who reports to the City Administrator, and so forth," they might think. "So, if I do an excellent job on my report, my division head will support it, and support it to his director, who will support it to her boss, and the Council will support it!"

It's a wonderful concept, and it can sometimes come true. However, it usually takes more than a good report to be an effective planner.

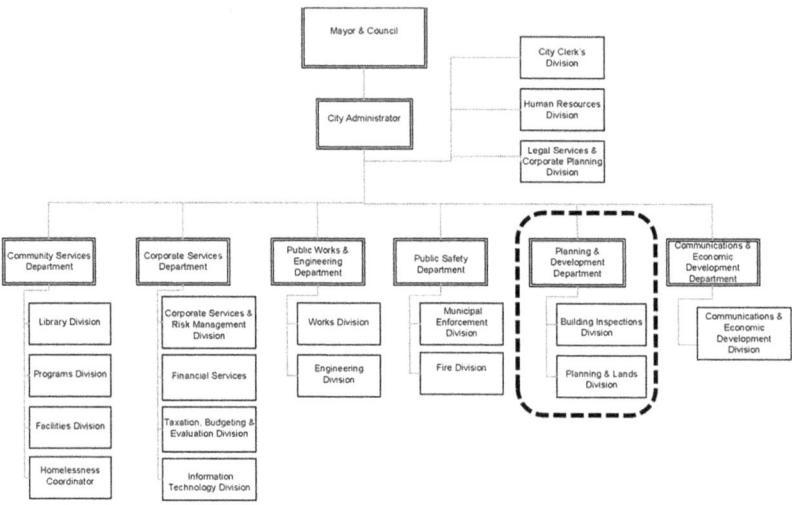

Figure 9.1 Organization chart. Credit: City of Yellowknife, NT, Canada, as modified by the author. Available at: https://www.yellowknife.ca/en/city-government/organizational-chart-of-city-departments.asp

Effective Planning Leaders

It's hard to think about effective planning leaders without running into some issues. Robert Moses was, for many years, the most effective planning leader in the United States. However, as was discussed earlier in this book, his other failings make it hard to look to him as a good example. Jane Jacobs was an effective leader in planning—so effective that she was able to lead away from Moses' path. However, much of her philosophy was based in the failings of the planning profession and the concept that planners should just leave things be.

Edmund Bacon in Philadelphia and Ed Logue in New Haven and Boston come closer to providing examples of planning leadership. However, neither of them was perfect. More recently, New Urbanist pioneers like Andres Duany showed a path forward with a positive model of planning. While it was often based in re-inventing planning from the ground up—a path that is rarely an option in typical cities—the example has merit.

It's understandable that many planners eschew leadership. Leading has a bit of a bad reputation in the planning world. Most often when people think of planners leading, they think about urban renewal. Planners led the way in efforts to destroy huge parts of cities in the name of progress. The idea of cleaning up slums and blight became an excuse to drive residents from their homes and to build large-scale, inhospitable buildings to replace them. Those large-scale projects were based on theories planners believed about urban regeneration and LeCorbusier's "Cities of Tomorrow." However, as the errors of those theories became clear in practice, it was the planners who had led these efforts that took the blame.

In the 1960s, planners were lumped in with everything that was wrong with society. In the name of "improvement," planners had led the way to more urban decay. Jane Jacobs, Robert Goodman, and many others castigated planners as intentionally undermining the urban fabric and culture in the name of a larger military-industrial complex.

In reality, most of these planners were probably interested in making the world a better place. They were likely horrified at the results of their work, as well as how they were perceived in popular culture. Planning as a profession retreated and regrouped, and a new generation of urban planners were trained in public participation methods and collaboration.

Figure 9.2 Radiant City. Credit: SiefkinDR. Creative Commons Attribution-Share Alike 4.0 International License, https://creativecommons.org/licenses/by-sa/4.0/legalcode

144 FIVE STEPS TO LEADERSHIP

Was this result inevitable? What might the planning profession have done differently in the 1950s to avoid this outcome and a half-century of suspicion from the very people they were aiming to help? The answer comes down to the difference between using raw power and leading.

Planners in the urban renewal era were given broad powers to condemn areas they deemed blighted and almost unlimited funds to build replacement buildings. There was no need to consult with the people affected. At the same time, the profession had little understanding about why they should ask people what they thought about these changes.

Not surprisingly, people fought back and the planners lost much of their power. Today, planning is often an administrative profession, where professional staff with graduate degrees do little more than draft staff reports and defer to political leaders and the public. Planners often grumble about this situation. At their worst, planners may wield the limited power they have in making an applicant jump through unnecessary hoops to get their signoff. At their best, they may simply be resigned to the situation and wait for payday.

Figure 9.3 Not even Fairbanks, Alaska, avoided large-scale urban renewal. Credit: Public domain photograph from the 1963 Lathrop High School Yearbook.

It doesn't have to be this way. There is a difference between the raw power exerted by urban renewal planners and true leadership in planning. There is definitely a difference between the administrative role played by most planners and leadership. How do planners get back to what they are supposed to do—providing the professional planning perspective on complex policy issues and suggesting solutions no one else can? By having the courage and empathy to listen to stakeholders—even angry stakeholders—and responding honestly and clearly. Sometimes this means that the planner has learned from the stakeholder. Just as often, the stakeholder may be missing an important perspective on the issues and needs to hear it. Finding that middle ground takes courage and self-confidence. It requires leadership.

The Great Communicator

Being a planning leader means being a good communicator. There's more than one way to explain the same information. How you choose to explain it can make the difference between making a new friend and making a mortal enemy.

Part of communicating well is finding the right way to say something. Using the right language means you can find common goals with lots of people, rather than just a select few who share a specific worldview. This can be the difference between leveraging the power of lots of people—some of whom are leaders in their own rights—and just working with a small set of advocates.

A non-planning example of this leadership lies in the coalition that formed to fight against the Axis powers in World War II. There is no doubt that the Allies disagreed on a number of basic things. The United States and the United Kingdom no doubt had major issues with the Soviet Union on matters ranging from human rights to the Soviet Union's early non-aggression pact with Germany. Even the United States and the United Kingdom had disagreements about issues, although these were not as significant. However, by 1941, the leaders of all three countries had decided that the Axis powers represented a major threat to all of them. They were able to set aside their differences and agree on a common goal that was communicated in the language that worked for each party.

Similarly, in planning, you can often find common goals with surprising allies. Affordable housing advocates can find common ground with Libertarians on reducing regulatory barriers to housing development. Conservationists can find common ground with those concerned about their own property values to reduce development potential on plots that to one party are a sensitive habitat and to the other simply represent a way to get a nice view.

As I will explain below, this finding of common goals is not without its challenges. You may not want to ally with a group that, in other areas that are important to you, hold views you can't support. Each individual has to find that comfort area where they are willing to make tradeoffs in order to be effective. However, it's very difficult to be an effective leader if you will not even consider making these tradeoffs.

How to Build an Alliance

Once you have decided that your big ideas are going to need help, you have to build that coalition that will help implement it. This is not as simple as explaining an idea at a planning conference, where everyone may agree it's a great idea.

In order to create an effective group to advance a good planning idea, you first have to conduct a fairly traditional stakeholder analysis. Who is likely to support your idea? Who may oppose it? Why might they have that view and how can you get potential supporters excited about it?

Once you know who may be supportive, you need to reach out to them. That may not always be possible in a complex political environment. You may need to pick your time and place carefully, and in some cases, you may not be able to meet directly. If you work for a Mayor who does not like a certain City Councilor, you may not want to meet with them, but you may be able to find a common friend who can communicate your ideas to them.

Once you (or someone else) have those meetings, the ideas need to be explained clearly and succinctly. They need to be phrased in plain English or, even better, in the terminology that person is familiar with in their own profession. Reducing the paved area may be a matter of improving stormwater quality to a wetlands scientist and a matter of becoming less car-dependent to a transit advocate.

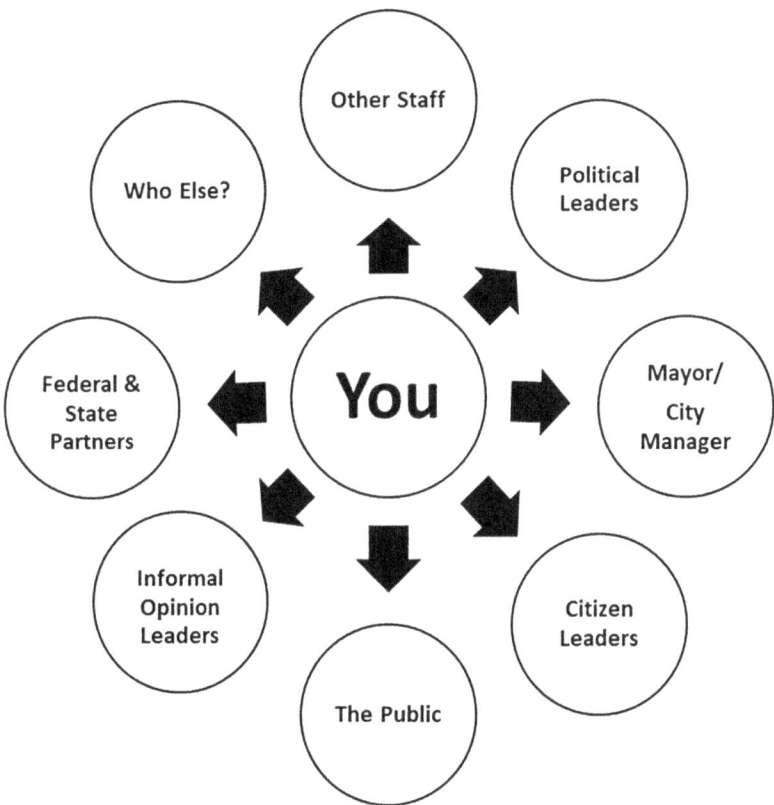

Figure 9.4 Thinking through stakeholders with whom you work. Credit: Author.

It's important to be engaged, even excited, without being overbearing. No one wants to have a discussion with a wide-eyed fanatic. And no one wants to have a discussion with someone who is boring and disengaged either.

Listen to what others are saying. Hear their concerns and ideas. You may have been wrong about their interest in supporting your ideas. On the other hand, you may realize your idea isn't so great after all. Good leaders are good listeners and adjust their plans accordingly.

Find common goals and acknowledge differences with others. You may have to reveal the 800-lb gorilla in the room, in the form of a major difference of opinion you may have with that person, in order to move beyond it. In the case of the City Councilor mentioned above, you may

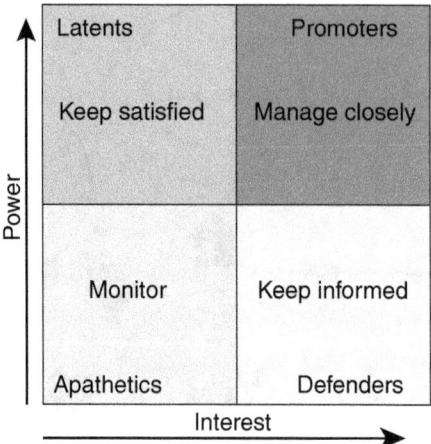

Figure 9.5 A Power-Interest matrix, showing strategies to use based on the quadrant in which the stakeholder is categorized. Credit: Zirguezi, https://commons.wikimedia.org/wiki/File:Stakeholders_matrix.svg

have to explain that, while you like working for the Mayor and like their leadership, this Councilor may not. This doesn't require a big discussion, but it's usually a good idea to get the difference on the table and then move beyond it to ideas you may both agree about.

There is more than one kind of community member and leader in this world. In fact, it's helpful to think of a matrix that divides them into four types based on the amount of power they have in the system and how much interest they have in your ideas. "Latent" stakeholders have the most power but the least interest. "Promoters" have both power and interest. "Apathetic" stakeholders have less of both, and "Defenders" have a high amount of interest but little power. Each can be useful in different planning debates—although, not surprisingly, some are more useful than others—and keeping in mind each style you may work with will help you in framing your big ideas.

Let's explore each of these groups in a bit more detail:

- *Latents.* These are powerful people if you can motivate them properly. Sometimes they are the people you know support a certain idea, but who aren't at the public meeting. Lots of *Defenders* and *Promoters* are there, so why aren't the *Latents?* This situation can be especially frustrating when you have spoken to them and you suspect they are a majority in the community. Even worse, they have spoken to your boss, but won't bother to come out publicly. Getting *Latents* motivated to get involved can be important to good leadership. In private settings, public relations firms are often charged with this task. In your public sector world, that's not usually an option and you and your staff have to serve that purpose.

- *Apathetics*. These may be the true majority of people if you are to believe much of what you hear about Americans nowadays. They just don't really care much about the issues that put a fire in your belly. Planning is meaningless to them. It's very hard to get them to be focused on your big ideas unless these are directly related to something they care about at that moment. For example, they may not care about environmental protection until someone proposes filling a wetland next to their house. Getting *Apathetics* engaged and supportive is a challenging aspect of planning leadership. Sometimes it is a lost cause. Sometimes you are able to find enough of a common interest with them to get support for ideas you want to champion. But be careful! That support can be fleeting. When they want to fill the wetland in their backyard to make space for a trampoline, suddenly they may not support environmental issues anymore!
- *Promoters*. These are the active and powerful section of the population. Whether fighting to protect their neighborhood, pushing for more affordable housing, or supporting good public transit, they put the "civic" in civic engagement. *Promoters* can be a great thing if they support ideas you want to lead on. If they are opposed, they can be your biggest challenge. Supportive *Promoters* need to be offered ways to help follow your lead—and most often they will. Ones who do not agree with you deserve engagement and discourse. They may not be convinced you are right, but the fact that you have discussed your ideas with them will often bring respect and deference from political leaders. Also, there may be some times you realize they have a point, and perhaps your leadership efforts should shift course a bit to resolve their concerns.
- *Defenders*. When people want to be *Promoters* but lack the influence or effectiveness, they are *Defenders*. Often on the short end of political

battles, but with strong opinions, they have the passion, but can't seem to score the big wins. However, occasionally *Defenders* will be a part of a winning coalition, as they sometimes can evolve into *Promoters*. Even if they don't, they are worth consulting on any big idea, if only because that's the right way to do planning. Sometimes they may surprise you with their willingness to do little things to follow your lead.

In general, the most effective planning leadership approach is to motivate the *Promoters* who support your lead and activate *Latents* who support your ideas, but may not bother to do anything unless you tell them what and how. In Figure 9.5 above, I suggest actions to utilize for each of these four types. Playing a game with a lot of players requires playing different hands for each of them. In planning, unlike in cards, that's allowed—as long as you remain honest at all times.

How Are You Viewed?

I've described how you identify various important members of a possible coalition. I've also talked about how some people may serve as your loyal opposition that you may not win over, but should engage with anyway. Now comes the next step, which has to do with making that link between wanting to have effective allies and actually having them.

Different Types of Stakeholders Require Different Approaches

This is a difficult part of the process because it involves some soul searching and even honesty about the role of planning in today's world. Doing so without defensiveness and with an open mind doesn't make you a bad leader; it makes you stronger.

Think about these various stakeholders: political leaders, neighborhood group presidents, other department heads, and others. Then think about what *they* think you do all day. Be as cynical as you can and try to sum it up in one sentence. Some examples may be as follows:

- *Neighborhood Leaders* think you try to destroy the livability of their neighborhoods by not *stopping* projects that are bad.

- *The City Manager or Mayor* may think you complicate important city projects by bringing up issues like historic preservation.
- *Other Department Heads* ideally think you help them get their jobs done. Sometimes they may not be sure what planners do all day except regulate.
- *Federal Partners* may think you conflate local priorities with federal ones. They may even think you don't keep good files when they come to audit your grant programs. Ideally, they think your work is an effective way to use federal funds on good local projects.

Some of these may be worst-case scenarios, but may help you think about how to frame your ideas for these people when you want them to follow your lead. To a city manager, you can emphasize how much smoother projects go when they factor in your planning issues ahead of time. To a federal partner, you can remind them that when you look good spending federal grants, they look good. This framing can pre-empt efforts to undermine your leadership with snarky comments or simple reluctance to engage with you on your initiatives.

Five Steps to Political Savvy

So, you know who you need to convince to follow your leadership, and even have some ideas about their personality types and what approach might be helpful to take in relation to dealing with them. There are five universal steps that will help you be an effective leader and allow you to have a good conversation with these members of your community:

1. *Reach out to them.* It takes time to build interpersonal relationships. You can't just start when you need someone's support; you have to show real interest and good listening skills. This takes time and effort. It may even involve opening up a little bit and adding a personal dimension. This is where planners who are more gregarious are at a big advantage. As you meet with people for a periodic coffee or at least a phone call, spend some time learning about their values and needs. By all means, meet with the neighborhood activist who doesn't seem to like you very much.

2. *Explain your perspective.* As you build this relationship, periodically explain what you hope to get done—not just in the moment, but in the long term. Have concepts that are compelling like "I want to make it easier to build the right things in our city and harder to build the wrong things." As part of this conversation, explain why you want their support. Be honest. Speak from your heart, not as a calculating bureaucrat. Tell this neighborhood activist why you support density in the neighborhood, at least sometimes.
3. *Acknowledge your differences.* Many people will have different views of the world from you. That's OK. It's important to recognize these differences and be upfront about them, so that you can get past them. Tell people that you may disagree on those issues, but you hope you can agree on certain common concepts. Be honest, but also focus on what you have in common. Be clear that you understand the activist does not support dense infill developments most of the time.
4. *Respect them.* Respect stakeholders' power. Tell them you know that they have some influence and you are hoping to get them to use that influence to help on the efforts you have in common with them. Don't be condescending. As you speak to stakeholders, keep in mind that you identified them for a reason and remember why. Tell that neighborhood activist that you know lots of people listen to them on planning issues and that you hope you can get them to support your ideas.
5. *Say their support matters.* This almost goes without saying, but explain why you want—maybe even need—their support to pull off your effort. Don't pander to them, but explain why it is important to you. Try to explain why working closely with you on this effort helps them as well. Tell the activist that you hope to gain their trust, if not agreement.

These five steps are not always going to be the same. You will probably not have time to follow them all with each person you need to support your efforts. On the other hand, as good planners know, you have to know what plan to deviate from. These five steps are the ideal plan to start from.

FIVE STEPS TO LEADERSHIP 153

Isn't This Just Empty Spin?

At this point, you may be wondering if you are reading a book about planning or a self-help narrative. Even worse, maybe you are wondering if you are reading a book on the ad business or even Soviet-era propaganda.

No, this is important for you as a planner. It's not the same as selling cigarettes or convincing citizens to work harder. You will be using some similar tools, but hopefully for a much more civic end. Rather than selling candy, you are selling ideas that will make your world a better place.

Figure 9.6 Using good leadership skills is not the same as doctors selling cigarettes! Credit: Collection of Stanford Research into the Impact of Tobacco Advertising, https://tobacco.stanford.edu

Figure 9.7 Nor is using good social skills to lead the same as pushing for the end of capitalism! Credit: Public domain in the U.S.

In Other Words…

Planners have lots of big ideas, but don't always spend time figuring out how to get people to care about them. Most often planners use their own language to describe ideas—an effective tool to get support from other planners, but not so much for political leaders or the public. Thinking about why others should care about your ideas is an important tool for leadership.

Leading is hard work. Once you have your big idea, the work has just begun. First you need to identify the stakeholders who may matter in implementing your idea. Then you need to figure out what kind of stakeholders they are. Finally, you need to spend a lot of time working with them to find common threads between what motivates them and where you want to lead. It's much more time-consuming than just sitting in a conference hearing about the new ideas in planning. On the other hand, you probably entered this profession to make a difference. This is the best way to make sure the difference you are making is the one you care most about.

CONCLUSION

Combing a Giant Hairball

Politician, technician, or hybrid?

Without thinking too much, where would you classify yourself? Where do you think planners should find their role? This question has been asked for over 40 years. Interestingly, the perception of the proper role of planners has changed over that time.

Where do planning leaders fit into these classifications? Are leaders inherently political?

In 1979, planning researchers Elizabeth Howe and Jerome Kaufman published their work on ethics in planning. (Howe and Kaufman 1979). They surveyed 616 planners and characterized them based on their responses to various ethical situations. Those who were seemingly viewing ethical choices differently based on whether they agreed with the end goal were dubbed "politicians." Those who viewed ethical choices strictly, whether they agreed with the end goals or not, were dubbed "technicians." A group of planners who fell somewhere in between were dubbed "hybrids."

For example, Howe and Kaufman asked planners whether the following situation was ethical:

> Suburban planner decides to organize support from local people to put pressure on suburb's officials to change community's exclusionary zoning policy [by organizing a] coalition of support to induce pressure… (Howe and Kaufman 1979, 244)

Just over half of the planners (53 percent) found that approach ethical. However, when cross-categorized with the classifications above, those seen as "politicians" were much more likely to view this strategy as ethical than those seen as "technicians":

> In general the politicians are more accepting of the political tactics in the scenarios than the technicians are, although this does not mean they think all tactics are ethical. (Howe and Kaufman 1979, 251)

This was the case despite their finding that planners "consider threat, distortion of information, and leaking of information as the most unethical tactics" (Howe and Kaufman 1979, 246).

While many planners fit into one of those two categories, they found that half of the planners surveyed were somewhere in between – the so-called "hybrids." These planners believed that one should be both technically sound and politically savvy:

> Initially, we thought that an important explanation for differences in ethical perceptions among planners could be traced to a central and continuing conflict in planning, how can planners maintain their technical integrity, yet at the same time be politically effective? Planning has been struggling over the question of its proper stance as a public profession in a democratic society for many years … The issue has often been posed as a choice between the polar models of the planner as technician … and the planner as a political actor … The former type is supposed to be technically expert, value neutral, and responsible to the public through the political decision-makers he serves. But he is also dependent on those same political

decision-makers for the implementation of his "good" advice and plans. The latter, as an ideal type, is more value committed, more responsive to the groups or issues he thinks are particularly related to the public interest, and more willing to work actively through the political system to see that plans are implemented. Only in recent years have there been attempts to think in terms of a role which combines aspects of both technical and political roles to achieve both integrity and effectiveness. (Howe and Kaufman 1979, 248–249)

This idea of the planner as neither politician nor technician emerged in the post-urban renewal era of the 1970s as a possible new ideal. The planner was not Robert Moses, a pure power-driven force who seeks to supplant political leaders. Neither was the planner the back-office worker attached to their computer, producing data without any context. The idea of the "hybrid" planner was a happy medium between the two:

[T]he role we have called the hybrids provides some new insight into the practice of planning, since these people are trying to bridge the gap, combining the characteristics of both roles … the interesting aspect of our study is that it is the hybrids who dominate, not the politicians; and it is the hybrids who make the greatest effort to combine both the technical and the political aspects of role. This would indicate that they are likely to be sensitive to both the problem of loss of legitimacy and the problem of lack of effectiveness. The two aspects of their role do involve a tension which may at times be difficult to balance. (Howe and Kaufman 1979, 253–254)

So, while the idea of the planner as hybrid is seen as potentially effective, it raised some interesting questions about how to guide the decision-making process when placed in that role. When do you decide to be political? When do you write a really good report to support a political figure's efforts? How much do you use data to suggest an action and how much do you just report the data?

Leaders as Hybrids

What does this have to do with leadership anyway? We haven't talked much about ethics or professional norms so far. That's because there is a reasonable assumption that you are a generally ethical person who tries to do the right thing.

The reason this research is relevant is that there are times in leading where you will inevitably have to wrestle with the issues studied in Howe and Kaufman's research. Leading isn't just about waiting for someone to take up your offer to provide advice. On the other hand, leading in planning is not the same as being a purely political leader. As discussed in Chapter 2 and again in Chapter 8, planning leaders have to think about how much to be guided by data and technical factors, and how much to move good ideas forward. As we described in Chapter 6, one part of the effort to lead involves guiding public opinion – without being dishonest.

It's important in planning to be guided by facts and data. That's what differentiates planning from many other fields – planners should come to a problem with an open mind and not attached to one solution. While there are good examples of best practices out there, we don't just cut and paste them into our communities. We adapt concepts based on data and experience. In that way we are technicians.

On the other hand, effective planning cannot just be based on a good report. We need interpersonal skills and a willingness to gently sell our good ideas once we figure them out. We need to be willing to converse with our natural foes and engage with hostile stakeholders, hopefully winning some of them over. We need to give compelling testimony at public meetings and convince City Councils and town meetings to vote for our ideas. In that way, we are politicians.

Leading in planning is therefore in keeping with the 50.3 percent of planners who saw themselves in that hybrid role. We need to be able to do both well. The goal of this book has been to help you determine when to do one and when to do the other.

Twenty-First-Century Update

A lot has changed since 1979. We don't wear bellbottoms to work. Of course, as I write this during the COVID-19 pandemic, many of us don't go "to" work at all, but work remotely. So maybe some of us are wearing bellbottoms again.

Certainly, the work environment for planners has changed since Howe and Kaufman's original research. Fortunately, in 2017, the researchers

Mickey Lauria and Mellone Long did some survey work and updated the 1979 study (Lauria and Long 2017).

Lauria and Long held focus groups and surveyed 1,334 planners who were members of the American Planning Association. They asked demographic questions, an updated version of the questions asked by Howe and Kaufman, and some additional questions about ethics. This survey provides an updated snapshot as to how the planners in the U.S. view their roles in the twenty-first century.

They asked a similar set of questions as Howe and Kaufman. For example, one question was:

> You are a city planner and one of your responsibilities is to maintain the planning department content on the City's Facebook page. The City has just recently obtained a Facebook presence and currently has very few policies on its use. A citizen requests a copy of an application in for development approval. (Lauria and Long 2017, 209)

In general, they found that the role of planners had changed since 1979. In their research, over half of planners now identified as "technicians" and only 10 percent as "hybrids." The number of "politician" planners went down slightly from 18 percent to 15 percent.

A new group had also emerged, which Lauria and Long described as "careerists." This group, making up one-fifth of all planners surveyed, was not especially interested in either the technical side or the political side of planning. They generally seemed satisfied with doing their job reasonably well and leaving the debate and analysis to others.

Lauria and Long summarized their findings in saying that "the political role of planners has diminished significantly: overtly in a drop in the politician role, but mostly by the decrease in the hybrid role offset by the corresponding increase in technicians" (Lauria and Long 2017, 210).

Why have there been these changes since the 1970s? Was it simply a change in what society expected from planners? Were planners just more interested in technical analysis and wanted to leave the politics to others? Certainly, many planners see politics as a dirty word. On the other hand, effective planning leadership requires some political actions. Are planners less interested in leading too?

Lauria and Long generally attribute this finding in part to the fact that more planners today do not have a planning background and therefore are less inclined to be mission-driven to success as planning leaders:

> The low number of politically oriented planners in our sample runs counter to the large percentage of executive level planners in our sample who are subject to higher levels of political influences. This unexpected finding suggests that our respondents may have been hesitant to admit to political influences on their professional ethics or that these professional planners were not planning educated. To evaluate this unexpected finding with the data we have, we cross-tabulate the roles that planners chose with their educational background; we find that 62% of the hybrid, and 63% of the political planners, were planning educated, while only 54% of the technicians were educated in planning programs (a statistically significant difference at the .05 level). Thus, the differences between the number of technical planners in our two samples may in fact be due partially to the increase in number of non-planning-educated practicing planners (e.g., civil engineers, economists, geospatial sciences, environmental engineers, etc.). (Lauria and Long 2017, 211)

They also find that those who do seek to play a political role are more likely to be young, at executive-level positions, or in the public sector. Perhaps, as planning processes that have grown more complicated over time, there are just more people working as planners who simply view it as a job rather than a chance to make changes in the world:

> We find, in updating the seminal 1979 Howe and Kaufman survey of practicing planners, that most planners today reject a political role as an advocate for specific policies or stakeholders, and are more likely to adopt a technician role as an unbiased professional simply reporting data and information to a variety of stakeholders. (Lauria and Long 2017, 218)

If this is true, planning today is still suffering from the sins of urban renewal. Planners (and non-planners who end up in planning positions) do not want to be in a role of leadership.

Except you, right? You want to be a planner leader and it looks like there is less competition than ever in the profession.

Hairball Combing

In 1996, Gordon MacKenzie, a long-time executive at Hallmark Cards, self-published a book on management, which had the imaginative title *Orbiting the Giant Hairball: A Corporate Fool's Guide to Surviving with Grace*. In it, he said that corporations become tangled and messy, like a hairball, because they relied on old systems and traditions. The book became so popular that it was published by Viking in 1998.

This concept is even more true in government organizations. The idea that "we've always done it this way" is a powerful one, because change in government is risky. If a new system doesn't work, the inventor of the system will get the blame. In private business, there is at least the incentive of making more money; in government, there is no such incentive.

With the documented increase in "careerist" planners, it's no wonder that most planning offices are giant hairballs. Unlike corporations, you can't just choose to move to another one if you don't like it. If you care about your community, there's likely only one government entity that plans for it. If it's a hairball, you have to deal with it.

MacKenzie suggested that you needed to get yourself away from all the hairs and resist the gravitational pull to be in the ball. By "orbiting," you become free to do your own thing and make good things happen.

This model applies to some extent in planning as well. You can't expect to make big changes in the community when you are bogged down in whether a sign meets your city's code. That's good work for someone to do and it matters. On the other hand, there are a lot of signs in the world.

However, if there is a problem with your sign code, a good planning leader can't ignore it. Your reputation is connected to how people perceive your office. If your sign code doesn't allow for interesting signs, a good leader works to fix it.

Rather than orbiting, planning leaders need to tackle the tough work of combing out that planning hairball. The hybrid in you understands both the complexity of making change and the need to keep the politics of a situation in mind. So, to stick with the sign code example for a moment, combing the hairball would mean fixing the code, but also making sure your fixes have some short-term positive effects that people notice.

Where Does This Leave You?

In this book we've looked at planning leadership from a number of perspectives. We've thought about the failings of early planning leaders, as well as some of their strengths (Chapter 1). We've looked at why you may want to lead (Chapter 2), running an office (Chapter 3), working with a boss (Chapter 4), working with the press (Chapter 5), and models of planning with others (Chapters 6 and 7). We also talked about thinking strategically (Chapter 8). Finally, we've looked at a few key things to think about when leading in planning (Chapter 9).

At some point, however, you just have to try to do the leadership thing. There's no way to get good at it without trying. You'll make mistakes, that's for sure. If you are careful, those mistakes will have few consequences and you'll learn from them. In the end, if you are the type of planner who wants to lead for better communities, you are going to have to take those risks.

Leading is a scary thing. No one is in front of you to show you the way you are going. If you are driven to make a difference in the world, you will be willing to take those steps and have other people follow. You can do it!

Bibliography

Howe, Elizabeth and Kaufman, Jerome. 1979. "The Ethics of Contemporary American Planners," *Journal of the American Planning Association* 45:3, 243–255. DOI: 10.1080/01944367908976965.

Lauria, Mickey and Long, Mellone. 2017. "Planning Experience and Planners' Ethics," *Journal of the American Planning Association* 83:2, 202–220. DOI:10.1080/01944363.2017.1286946.

MacKenzie, Gordon. 1998. *Orbiting the Giant Hairball: A Corporate Fool's Guide to Surviving with Grace.* New York: Viking.

AFTERWORD

I finished writing this book in a different world from the one in which I began writing it. Likely, by the time you read it, things will have changed again. Pandemic, an awakening awareness of the prejudices built into our society, and the backlash from the far right have all led us to a difficult place as a nation. People are edgy, and many people are stuck at home with their roommates or family with not a lot of information about when the situation may change. Closer to home, I have changed my professional role, changing how I perceive the nature and goals of the planning profession.

Of course, we've been in tough places before. Certainly, the years leading up to the Civil War, or the onset of the Great Depression, or even the Cold War created challenges for our country and our world. In each case, leaders emerged who helped guide us through these challenges.

These leaders were not perfect. We didn't agree with everything they did. However, they provided a bedrock of sorts for most of society to rest their foundations upon. When we criticize these leaders—often rightfully—we are not usually saying they didn't help us immeasurably when they led us through uncertain times. We are simply pointing out things they could have done differently.

Planning is an introspective profession. We often analyze situations—some might say over-analyze them—and have a penchant for finding the "perfect solution."

There really aren't many perfect solutions.

If you are a typical planner, your willingness and ability to lead may be held back by your professional instincts. You may want to lead and fear that you will make the wrong decision, or you may not be able to make up your mind as to how to move forward.

In the end, though, the role of a leader is to make decisions in a timely fashion, with the best data available. That doesn't mean you won't make mistakes; in fact, you almost certainly will. I wouldn't say you should make mistakes, but if you make tough decisions, they won't always be correct.

Earlier we talked about policy windows, those limited opportunities to move forward on an issue dear to your heart. If you miss the policy window, you may have lost your chance to make something happen. These policy windows open based on political leaders, external events, and even some random events. As tragic as the killing of George Floyd was, it clearly provided a policy window to consider substantive changes in how race relations are governed in this country.

Not every policy window is navigated successfully. In 1993, President Bill Clinton saw an opening to enact healthcare changes. That policy window opened and closed without any healthcare reforms.

Why circle back to this somewhat abstract concept now, when you are almost done with this book? Because your interest in leading for substantive changes in how planning is done in this world depends on your willingness to act when the policy window opens. You will have a limited time to move forward and you may not have time to do all the analysis that planners typically relish. You'll need to take a deep breath and figure out how to do as much as you can to take advantage of the opportunity.

This is one of the failings of my beloved profession. Planners love data, maps, and looking at case studies for best practices. We get lost in map libraries and read every article we can find on parking requirements. I once agonized for weeks about the files in our office storage relating to urban renewal programs from 50 years ago. We were moving and I needed to decide how many of the files to keep. My planners' instinct was to keep all of them. In lieu of being able to do that, I started to pore over the individual papers—relocation reports, documentation of the condition of long-gone two-family homes, and federal grant receipts. I love that kind of material, and couldn't decide what to keep and what could be disposed of.

In that case, my policy window of sorts was the impending move date. I had to make some broad-brush decisions and move on. I decided which kinds of files we could move and which ones were headed for the recycling bin. Did I miss some good material for future urban historians? Almost certainly. On the other hand, I was able to get back to the office and back to the pressing needs of the day.

If you want to lead, you can't be on the floor of the storage room going through files. You need to go upstairs and get into the room where it happens.

INDEX

Note: Figures are indexed in *italic* page numbering, tables in **bold** page numbering.

action programs 108
activists 8, 152
"Advocacy and Pluralism in Planning" 104
advocate planners 9, 102–3, 107–8, 110, 112, 114, 118
affordable housing 25, 45, 60, 63, 88, 103, 111, 135, 146, 149
agencies 3, 13, 49, 51, 82, 86, 104–5, 127–9
agreements 31, 106, 114, 116–17, 122, 124, 138, 152
American Bar Association 117, 125
American Planning Association 160
applicants 46, 48–9, 75, 87, 90–1, 135, 137
applications 46, 90–1, 160; completed 91; current 91; electronic 50; reviewing 32; student 33
Axis powers 145

back-office workers 158
Backoff, Robert 136
Bacon, Edmund 17, 22–4, 27, 102, 142; a planner at heart 21; provides a road-map for planning leadership 17; shows respect for the existing built form 17; on a skateboard 23
The Battle for Gotham: New York in the Shadow of Robert Moses and Jane Jacobs 14
benefits 48, 90–1, 105, 127–9, 132, 139; of advocate planning 104; positive 90; of strategic planning 127, 135
Benson-Kenanav, Jesse 26–7
A Better Cambridge (YIMBY group) 27
biases 11, 69, 85, 105
bikers 68
births 141

INDEX

boards 2, 71, 92, 96–7, 116, 126, 136; high-maintenance 134; independent 96; local 32; members 97; public 96, 110
bosses 4, 30, 33, 35, 55–6, 60–3, 65–7, 69–77, 83, 96, 129, 132–3, 141, 149, 163; bad 53; and the board of directors 139; direct 90; and stakeholders 30
Boston 17–18, 20–1, 27, 142; area 26; downtown 19; mayor John Collins 19; region 122
Boston Redevelopment Authority 18–19, 28
BRA *see* Boston Redevelopment Authority
Breaking Robert's Rules 122
Brookline, Massachusetts 17, 124
Bryson, John 127–9, 132, 139
budgets 41, 51–2, 58, 115, 135; preparation 58; process 51; professional development 55
buildings 20, 43–5, 104, 106, 110, 115–17, 124, 128; church 124; eight-unit apartment 44; historic 22, 43, 45, 68, 80; inhospitable 143; landmarked 16; new apartment 110; new eight-unit 44; public 62; renovated 45; replacement 144; tall 27, 115
businesses 74, 106, 134, 137, 153, 162; downtown 134; and strategic planning as a tool for 135–6

Cambridge, Massachusetts 27–8
candidates 54
capitalism *154*
care *see* healthcare
careers 11, 13, 17–18, 21–2, 24, 27, 33, 40, 49, 61, 103, 119, 121; advice regarding 70; and making the "right" decisions 35; and management 44; and planning 34, 41, 87

Caro, Robert 14
cars 2, 68, 75, 126–7
Chambers of Commerce 73, 89, 91
charts, organizational 71, 73, 141
Checkoway, Barry 103
childcare providers 95
churches 124–5
cigarettes *153*
cities 1–2, 9, 15–16, 19, 25–8, 31–2, 61, 66–9, 83–4, 90–1, 98–9, 108–9, 111, 119–20, 142–3; functioning of 16; large 124; leaders 31–2; managers 61, 69, 72, 151; and the pandemic 1–2, 50, 164
"Cities of Tomorrow" 143
City Councilors 36–7, 61, 72, 146–7
City Councils 3, 52, 60, 63, 81, 90, 96–7, 159
City of Somerville's Assembly Square Planning Study (2000) *120*
city staff 69, 118–20
Cleveland City Planning Commission 109–10
Cleveland Policy Plan *109*, 110
"Cleveland Policy Planning Report" 108, *109*, 112
climate change 24–5
Clinton, Pres. Bill 165
coalitions 145–6, 150, 157
codes 32, 44–5, 48, 107, 163
CoLab *see* Community Innovators Lab
collaborations 21–2, 143
Collins, John 19–20
common goals 145–7
communication skills 6, 81
communicators 80, 82, 145
community 2, 4, 20, 30–3, 37, 39, 61–2, 71, 73, 94–5, 97, 102–3, 118–19, 138–9, 162; activists 24, 67, 70; alienated 101; changes 38; dispute resolution 122;

engagement 108; groups 70; leaders 94; members 70, 122, 148; new 20; organizations 38; planners 84; wealthy 124
Community Innovators Lab 37–8
companies, private 86, 136–7, 163
compromises 19, 22, 111–12, 114
conflicts 33, 56, 63–5, 102, 114, 120–1, 123, 125, 133, 157; avoiding 76; between interested parties 116; handling 56; local land-use 118; mediating 113; planning 124; with the policy direction of political leaders 89, 93
Consensus Building Handbook 122
Consensus Building Institute 120
corporations 163; *see also* private companies
Councils 3, 31, 34–6, 84, 141; *see also* City Councils
courts 102, 117
culture 25, 92, 143
customer service 48, 84–7, 98, 137
customers 82, 85–6, 137; retail 85; satisfied 136; unwilling 86

Davidoff, Paul 102–5, 107, 112; advocate planners 9, 102–3, 107–8, 110, 112, 114, 118; believed that planners should listen to the needs of the community 102; concerned with low-income minority communities 103; founded the Suburban Action Institute 103; lawyer and city planner by training 102; proposed that planners should bring their own values of inclusiveness and positive change in order to support residents' needs. 102; published "Advocacy and Pluralism in Planning" 104

The Death and Life of Great American Cities 8, 111
decisions 13, 34–5, 43, 46, 53, 56, 69, 94, 96, 102, 113, 117, 136, 165; broad-brush 167; and decision makers 23, 129; difficult 46; final 34; financial 35; policy 133; ultimate 102; wrong 165
democracy 14, 92
Deputy Directors 34–5, 75–6
design 22, 44, 56, 68–9, 108, 122, 137; changes 44; issues 90; urban 22, 80, 108, 119
developers 31–2, 44–5, 74, 81, 91, 94, 112, 115–16, 118, 124; making reasonable design changes 44; non-profit 124; paying their fair share 74
development 20, 22, 24–7, 31–2, 44, 63, 81, 83, 90, 94, 112, 119–20, 146; agreements 31; approvals 160; better-planned 90; good 91; infill 17, 25, 83; initiatives 27; issues 27, 121; job-producing 43; large 62; mixed-use 119; new 25, 27, 43–4, 62; projects 31; review process 130; sites 89
difficult employees 47
directors 28, 34, 136, 139, 141
dispute resolution community 122
disputes 116–17, 124, 133; between parties 114; land use 115; planning 121
dissonance and synergy between the priorities of the planner and the mayor 65
documents 8, 39, 48, 57, 89, 104; electronic 51; iterative 38; public 39, 89; written 38
Doonesbury cartoon 11
downtown 19, 60, 94, 98, 105–6; area 44, 63, 83; buildings 83; businesses 134; parking 106
Driscoll, Kim 61

drivers 68–9
Duany, Andres 142
Dunkelman, Marc J. 16–17

elected officials 62
Employee Assistance Programs 48
employees 46, 48–50, 54–8, 76, 95, 141; bad 53; current 55; difficult 46, 47, 48, 56; essential 2; flex-time 53; good 41, 46, 53–5; long-time 47; motivated public 51; preferences coming to light during the pandemic 50
employers 34, 49, 104
environment 25, 44, 46, 50, 77; changing 127; complex local 36; current planning 15; external 98, 130; interdisciplinary 2; political 5, 76, 146; public sector 51; rural 79; urban 49
environmental issues 121, 149
environmental protection 74, 88, 149
Envision Cambridge (city-wide plan) 27
equity (concept) 9, 19, 21, 25–6
ethics 158, 160, 163; in planning 156; professional 107, 161
European cities 18; *see also* cities
Executive Directors 132

"facilitative leadership" 113–25
Fairbanks, Alaska 144
feedback 57
files 89, 166–7
Flint, Anthony 15
Floyd, George 165
focus groups 160
food chain 72–3
Forester, John 113, 118, 121, 123, 136
funding organizations 13, 51–2, 135, 137–8

global environmental issues 121
goals 33, 39, 62–3, 75, 78, 82, 108–9, 113, 127, 129, 134–5, 156, 159, 164; common 145–7; core 101; laudable 93; organizational 135; policy 76; primary 53, 116; strategic 89
Goldman, Lawrence P. 19
Goodman, Robert 8, 143
government 16, 34–6, 69, 71, 77, 82, 100, 122, 124, 126, 136, 162; agencies 47; local 52, 84; offices 135; organizations 82, 89, 163; planners 84; programs 111; small-town 124
Government Center Program 19
Governors 11, 74–5
Gratz, Roberta 14
Greene, Dick 20
groups 26, 38, 103, 105, 109, 113, 119, 132, 138, 146, 148, 156, 158, 160; effective 146; local neighborhood 83; new 161; strategic management 136–7; strong stakeholder 136; workshops 38; YIMBY 26–7

health, public 2–3, 50
healthcare 43, 51, 55, 63, 65–7, 77, 95, 111, 141, 149, 154–5, 162; changes 165; reforms 165
Heller, Gregory 24
highways 11, 21; *see also* roads
historic buildings 22, 43, 45, 68, 80
homes 25, 34, 51, 94–5, 101, 143, 164
housing 17, 20, 25–6, 65, 83, 106, 111–12, 121, 124, 136; affordable 25, 45, 60, 63, 88, 103, 111, 135, 146, 149; costs 26; deteriorated 108; developed 20; developments 146; infill 3;

low-income 124; managers 44–5; mixed-income 124; working-class 20; year-round 79
Howe, Elizabeth 156, 160
hubris, post-World War II 10, 14
"hybrid" planners 156–8, 160

ideas 4–5, 22–3, 25–7, 32–4, 60–1, 72–3, 76–7, 98–9, 107–8, 117–18, 128, 138, 146–52, 154, 158–59; exchanging of 49; "NIMBY" 25–6; planting in the public realm 73; supporting 149; volunteering 131
industrial development 20
infill development 17, 25, 83
information 1–2, 84–5, 95–6, 105, 110, 117, 145, 157, 161, 164; clear 86; complete 88; good 92, 97; important 91
intellectual peers 9
interests 21, 26, 39–40, 43, 45, 74, 76, 97, 102, 104, 111, 117, 119–20, 124, 147–8; common 149; public 158; reviving 138
interior designers 49
interpersonal relationships 4, 151
interviews 19, 34, 54, 88, 121, 140; of candidates 54; personal 28

Jacobs, Harvey 138
Jacobs, Jane 8, 9, 10, 11, 13–17, 21, 24–5, 28, 101, 111–12, 138–9, 142–3
Journal of the American Planning Association 103–4

Kaufman, Jerome 156, 160
Kennedy, John F. 124
Knope, Leslie 51
Knowles, Scott Gabriel 21–2
Kreiger, Alex 15
Krumholz, Norman 108, 110

labor complaints 41
labor relations 46
land 25, 81, 108
land use disputes 115
land use planners 141
landowners 83
languages 81, 105, 145, 154
Lauria, Mickey 160–1
laws 14, 55, 75, 82, 89, 91, 102
lawsuits 120–1, 124
lawyers 102, 105, 115, 117
leaders 4, 6–7, 27, 32, 35–7, 39–40, 73–4, 89–90, 94–5, 123–4, 129, 132–3, 135–6, 145, 164–5; approach 32; bad 150; better 29, 36, 40, 111; effective 82, 142, 146, 151; excellent 11; good 6, 27, 40, 60, 80, 147; long-term 52; military 123; of state 120; talented 128
leadership 2, 4–5, 10, 22, 26, 29, 40–1, 50, 55–6, 83, 87, 89, 126–55, 158, 162–3; challenges 59; collective 133; effective 58; efforts 60, 149; eschewed by planners 142; good 5, 149; interests 71; and managing staff 31; models 5, 123; NIMBY (Not in my Backyard) 25, 26; opportunities 95; in planning 145; political 89, 120; professional 52; public 137; qualities 34; risks 89; roles 13, 37, 133, 141, 163; skills 153; structures 141; YIMBY (Yes in my Backyard) 25, 26
LeCorbusier 143
legacies 14
legal cases 102
LeGates, Richard 102
Lend-Lease program 66
libertarians 146
listeners 4, 37, 114, 147
Logue, Edward J. 17–22, 24, 27, 142

Long, Mellone 161
low-income developments 20
low-income housing tax credits 111
low-income minority communities 103
low-income residents 19

MacKenzie, Gordon 162
management 5, 29, 42, 52, 69, 89, 163; careers 44; concepts 42; good document 88; human resource 135; leaders 141; physics 66; programs 36; public 42; responsibilities 136
managers 6, 30, 32, 42, 46, 49, 55, 59, 69, 76, 135; good 6, 29, 41–2, 69, 126; mid-level 56; no-nonsense 46; political 74; senior 66
managing 5, 42–3, 58, 61–78, 84, 89; and leading staff 31; money 42, 58, 59; people 42, 59; priority issues 137; programs 42, 59; staff 31; stakeholders 137
"managing up" skills 4, 69
Massachusetts 17, 27, 61, 119–20, 124
Massachusetts Institute of Technology 37–8, 121
Mayors 20, 61, 63, 65, 74, 83, 90–1, 108, 121, 134, 146, 148, 151; bans of 24; prioritizing issues 64; signing-off 77; strong 61, 136; and their administrations 110
media 4, 24, 80, 87, 95–7; local 69; modern 95; relations 82, 88; training exercises 80
mediation 114, 115, 116–18, 120–5; activist 122–3; assessing potential 119; assessment 120–1; between parties 118; of conflicts 113; planning 5; processes 114, 121; public disputes 122; services 122–3

mediators 113, 115–19, 122–3; claiming pure neutrality 122; conducting the process in joint session 117; and public disputes 122; skilled 114–16
memos 3, 7, 57, 97
migrations 141
mistakes 9, 19, 27, 163, 165
MIT *see* Massachusetts Institute of Technology
models 84, 102, 118–19, 123, 138, 141, 162–3; leadership 5, 123; of planning 102, 164; polar 157; positive 142
money 13, 22, 33, 41, 58, 63, 126, 162
Moses, Robert 12, 14–17, 19, 24, 102, 142, 158; command-and-control style 21; fall from power 14; leadership style 14–15; legacy 15; strengths of 12; tactics 15
"Mystic View Task Force" 119–20

negotiating parties 122
neighborhoods 3, 11, 19–21, 63, 73, 83–4, 110–11, 118, 134, 149–50, 152; activists 151–2; declining 108; planning process 130; residents 19, 80, 83; and their leaders 150; urban 14; using checks on government 16
neighbors 25, 45, 115, 124–5
neutrality 6, 122
New Jersey Performing Arts Center 19
New York City 14–17, 20–1, 28, 102, 163; parks and public pools 14; politics of patronage 11; and quasi-public agencies 13; transportation 11; urban renewal efforts of the mid-twentieth century 11
New York Times Review of Books 14
New York Urban Development Corporation 20

NIMBY (Not in my Backyard) 25–6
"non-planners" 106, 162
nonpartisanship 122
nonprofit and community-based planners 84
Nutt, Paul 136

office 4–5, 31, 41–60, 62, 74–5, 79, 85–6, 90, 93, 98–9, 126, 134–5, 137, 162–3, 166; buildings 19; complex 58; large 41; layouts 49–50; managing 58; private 41; professional 98; storage 165
officials, elected 62
Ogden, William 14
open floor plans 50
open spaces 22, 26, 125, 140
opposition 105, 107; intolerance of 14; loyal 150; plans 105
"orbiting" (concept) 162–3
Orbiting the Giant Hairball: A Corporate Fool's Guide to Surviving with Grace 156, 162–3
organizational 37, 71, 73, 92, 94, 127–30, 135, 139, 141–2; charts 71, 73, 141; competence 92; culture 92; missions 94; strengths 130
organizations 30, 33–4, 40, 48, 51, 53–4, 70, 74, 77–8, 82–3, 86, 89, 93–5, 103, 127–37; changes 129; charts 142; community 38; funding of 13, 51–2, 135, 137–8; government 82, 89, 162; international 121; local 121; mission and values 130, 134; nonprofit 127, 139; private 86, 104; third-sector 139
Ouroissoff, Nicolai 16
outreach process 69

pandemic 1–2, 50, 165
parking 69, 80–1, 83, 98, 106
"parklets" 98, 99
parks 11, 14, 22, 24, 67, 80–1, 106

Penn Station, New York 16
pensions 77
personal theory of practice 38–9
personal values 38
personalities 13, 46, 65
perspectives 14, 47–8, 56, 74, 114, 130, 152, 164; participatory 18; positive 14–15; professional planning 145
Philadelphia 17, 22, 24, 27–8, 142
"planner arrogance" (concept) 11
planners 2–4, 6–11, 21–3, 39–43, 49–50, 65–7, 80–2, 98–9, 101–7, 110–14, 116–19, 140–5, 153–4, 156–63, 165–6; agency 104; careerist 162; castigated 143; developing common solutions 81; dislike of 8; economic development 43; executive level 161; "hybrid" 156–8, 160; modern 21; municipal 107; nonprofit and community-based 84; and plans 108; political 160–1; professional 10, 39, 97, 161; public-sector 136–7; publicly oriented 136, 161; role of 156, 160; seasoned 113; strategic 136; strong 17; suburban 157; technical 161; town 124; transportation 43, 141; urban 22, 143; young 24, 26, 79–80, 111
planning 22, 108, 126–7, 138; careers 34, 41, 87; communities 110; conflicts 124; expertise 3, 32; goals 4, 21, 30, 83, 141; management 29–30; organizations 50, 139; professionals 52; professions 5–6, 8–9, 16, 30, 101, 122, 142, 144, 164; programs 5, 8, 161; projects 11, 33; research 106; tools 70, 72, 91, 106, 138M NM
Planning Boards 3, 37, 83, 89, 91, 94, 96, 115–16, 119
Planning in the Face of Conflict 114

planning leadership 10, 13, 17, 22, 24, 75, 97, 142, 149, 163; effective 162; twentieth-century 17
planning offices 5, 43, 46, 50, 58, 74, 82, 85, 124, 126, 135, 137, 162; local government 33, 46; municipal 61
plans 13, 16, 20, 22, 24, 27, 44–5, 72, 91–2, 102–5, 108, 111, 129–30, 132, 157–8; city's 32; competing 102; comprehensive 8; developing 24; ideal 152; local 27; long-range 1; master 96; preparing 104; revised 44; strategic 130
plural planning 104–5
pluralism 103–4, 112
policies 5, 32, 44–5, 57, 86, 89–90, 108, 160–1; changing community's exclusionary zoning 158; goal changing 76; organization's media 87; personnel 57
"policy plans" 108, 110
"policy windows" 65, 98–9, 165–6
political appointees 74–5
political decision-makers 158
political environment 5, 76, 146
political roles 159, 161–2
politicians 2, 12–13, 17, 96, 156–59
politics 11, 28, 33, 43, 66, 80, 94, 141, 160, 163
Portland 27, 68; "parklet" in 99; society of architects 68
positions 5, 13, 30, 35, 55, 61–2, 70–1, 75, 85, 87, 96, 104; administrative 54; executive-level 161; full-time 33; long-held 22; top-level leadership 36
post-World War II hubris 10, 14
power 5, 13–14, 17, 19, 22, 73, 77, 109, 117, 125, 136, 139, 144–5, 148, 152; devolving 16; imbalances 122; limiting 49, 144; public 16; raw 144–5; structures 4, 6, 73, 141; yielding 3
The Power Broker 14, 16
Power-Interest Matrix 148
press 95, 163; *see also* media
The Principles of Scientific Management 127
priorities 52, 65, 76–7, 92; changing 65; key 76; local 151; strategic 136
private companies 86, 136–7, 162
private sector 51–2, 85, 89, 135, 137–9; customer services 85; leaders 139; offices 51; union membership 52
problems 43, 46, 49, 74, 80, 86, 91, 98, 101, 105–6, 108, 114, 134, 158–59, 163; current 134; growing 101; real 10, 25; worsening 48
process 4–5, 38–9, 47, 49, 85, 87, 89–90, 102–3, 105–7, 111–13, 117, 121–2, 124, 128–30, 133–7; basic 131; communal 129; decision-making 128, 159; natural 111; permitting 89, 91; political 103–4; private 117; review 115
profession 2–4, 6, 10, 21, 32–3, 40, 101, 104–5, 108, 111, 143–4, 146, 155, 162, 165; administrative 144; interactive 50; introspective 165; legal 117; public 157
professional 18, 38, 70, 122; administrators 61; advice 79; conduct 57; goals 37–9, 51; instincts 52, 166; practices 38, 76; relationships 97; reputation 41; roles 20–1, 164
programs 5, 19, 30, 32, 48, 59, 89, 103, 105, 111, 122, 126; graduate 25; grant 151; housing rehabilitation 89; housing voucher 111; logistics 2; master's 32

projects 11–13, 15–17, 19–20, 31–2, 44–6, 54–5, 77, 83, 85, 90–1, 96, 106–7, 115, 124–6, 150–1; clearance 19; large-scale 101, 143; municipal 63; new 85; redevelopment 119; reviewing 91; seven-unit 45
promoters 148–50
protection, environmental 74, 88, 149
PTOP *see* personal theory of practice
public agencies 3, 51, 86, 104–5, 127–9
public health 2–3, 50
public office 5, 41, 43, 51, 53, 61, 85, 87, 137–8
public officials 61–2, 96
public opinion 79–83, **84**, 85–100; influencing 84; leading 79–99
public planning offices 135
public pools 14; *see also* swimming pools
public sector offices 51, 74, 135
public transit 25, 29, 75, 149
publications 16, 122; *The Battle for Gotham: New York in the Shadow of Robert Moses and Jane Jacobs* 14; *Breaking Robert's Rules* 122; *Consensus Building Handbook* 122; *The Death and Life of Great American Cities* 8, 111; *Orbiting the Giant Hairball: A Corporate Fool's Guide to Surviving with Grace* 156, 162–3; *Planning in the Face of Conflict* 114; *The Power Broker* 14, 16; *The Principles of Scientific Management* 127; *Robert Moses and the Modern City: The Transformation of New York* 15; *Robert Moses: Builder for Democracy* 14

quality controls 74
quarantine 1–2
questions 36, 159; demographic 161; hard 32; media's 96; personal 38; professional 39; provocative 38; theoretical 43

Radiant City 143
Reagan, Pres. Ronald 72
recruiting candidates 54
redevelopment 119–20; efforts in New York's Roosevelt Island 20; fast 119; large-scale projects 19; mixed-use 121
relationships, interpersonal 4, 151
reporters 79–81, 83–4, 87–8, 96; aggressive 79; and media training exercises 80
reports 4, 61, 90, 106–8, 126, 139, 141, 158; "Cleveland Policy Planning Report" 108–9, 112; high quality 141, 159–60; relocation 167; staff 7, 74, 76, 106, 126, 144
reputation 41, 46, 69, 89, 162
research 57, 73, 105–6, 159–60; Howe and Kaufman 159; planning 106
residents 13, 15, 26–7, 31, 81, 84, 86, 90, 94, 99, 104, 106, 109–12, 115, 119; active 60, 120; average 105; connected 67; driven from their homes 143; favorite 84; subdivision 115
resources 11, 32–3, 38, 118, 122, 124, 133, 137; federal 14; limited 58, 109; mobilizing 5, 137
responsibilities 30, 34, 48, 104, 109, 123, 161; democratic 82; management 136; statutory 51; work 66
risks 6, 35, 37, 50, 71, 84, 92–3, 96, 129, 163; level of **84**; low 83, 92; project's 77; real 43

roads 26, 68, 80
Robert Moses and the Modern City: The Transformation of New York 15
Robert Moses: Builder for Democracy 14
Rogers, Cleveland 14
Roosevelt, Pres. Franklin D. 65
Roosevelt Island 20

Saint Aidan's church (during construction) 123
sidewalks 32, 62, 69, 81
skateboarding 23–4
skeptics (corporate strategic planning) 138–9
skills 4–6, 35–6, 49, 54, 59, 66, 70, 86, 114, 133; admiring Moses' survival 13; basic crowd management 131; communication 6, 81; good listening 151; interpersonal 114, 159; leadership 127; social 154; technical 34, 54
slum clearances 14, 19
SMG *see* strategic management group
social media 8, 91–4
social skills 154
Somerville, Massachusetts 119–20
Soviet Union 72, 145
Spring Street 68–9
staff 42–3, 49–50, 53, 55–7, 59, 69, 72, 74, 76–7, 90–3, 98, 119, 128, 134, 137; front 50; meetings 60; planners 56; professional 74, 144; reports 7, 74, 76, 106, 126, 144; senior 136
stakeholders 21, 30, 33, 67, 70, 118, 121, 136–7, 145, 147, 148, 150, 152, 154, 161; apathetic 148; external 77; hostile 145, 160; latent 148–50; requiring different approaches 150

standards 22, 57, 107, 115
state agencies 51
state planning offices 75
Stokes, Carl 108, 110
Stout, Frederic 102
strategic conversations 127
strategic management 132–4, 136–7, 139; groups 136–7; processes 136–7, 139
strategic planning 5, 126–9, 132–5, 138–9; concept of 136; corporate 138; implementing 127; leaders 133; and leadership 127–39; model 132; paradox of 128; process 128–30, 132–4
Strategic Planning for Public and Nonprofit Organizations: A Guide to Strengthening and Sustaining Organizational Achievement 127
strategic priorities 136
strategic thinking 30, 134
strategies 5, 12, 19, 75–6, 94, 104, 111, 118, 122, 130, 137, 148, 157; alternative 73; common 118; economic 2; high-priority 137; personal leadership 112; toxic waste cleanup 122
streetscape 83, 108
suburban planners 158
support 24, 27, 45, 48, 55–6, 65–7, 72–3, 83, 88, 106–7, 141, 146, 148–52, 154, 157–8; political 103; public 65, 82; residents 102; strong 128; of YIMBY efforts 25
supporters 70, 107, 138
Susskind, Larry 121–3
Susskind's Consensus Building Institute 122
swimming pools 12, 14
SWOT analysis 130–1, 135
synergy and dissonance between the priorities of the planner and the mayor 65

systems 2, 40, 86, 89, 91, 141, 148, 162; adversarial 102; current planning 37; evaluative 105; formal 58; mechanical 126; multimodal transportation 140; political 159; transit 14, 26

Taft, Seth 108
teams 2, 30, 54–5, 70, 77–8, 133–5; communication 1–2; legal 45; members 30; players 3, 75; strategic management 137
technicians 157–62
tools 5, 10, 38–9, 82, 91, 110, 115, 135, 153; complex zoning 24; effective 154; important 154; interactive Web-based 91; mapping 80; private sector 137
traffic 25, 80, 90
transit 12, 32, 60, 146; corridors 26; dependency 110; good 79; important 79; improved 81, 83; policies 93; public 25, 29, 75, 149
transportation planners 43, 141
trust 23, 33, 67, 70, 72, 75, 152
TV reporters 96; *see also* media
Twitter 84, 92–3

union busters 46
unions 46–7, 52–3, 57; membership by sector 52; representatives 46; stewards 47
United Kingdom 145
United States 142, 145
units 44–5, 124; affordable 44–5, 111; extra 44; housing 111; low-income 124

universities 23, 28, 102, 114, 125, 127, 139
urban design 22, 80, 108, 119
urban renewal 3, 9, 14, 18–19, 21–2, 25, 68, 101, 110, 138, 143, 163; areas 119; avoiding large-scale 144; efforts 11, 19, 21; era 17, 111, 144; failures 68; Fairbanks, Alaska 144; leaders 110; movement 10; old-school 111; planners 145; plans 17, 119; professionals 18; programs 167; projects 9, 17, 102; Spring Street before 68; in the West End of Boston 18, 19

vaccines 1–2
values, personal 38
vectors 63–6
visionaries 61
voluntary compliance (with laws) 82

walkers 68
work environment 51, 141, 160
work responsibilities 66
workers 46–7, 50, 55, 77; back-office 158; incumbent 56; solid 54
workspaces 43, 49–50, 54, 73
World War II 18, 65, 145

YIMBY (Yes in my Backyard) 25–6

Zoll, Sam 61
zones 31–2
zoning 27, 32, 83, 108, 115
Zoning Board of Appeals 96

For Product Safety Concerns and Information please contact our EU
representative GPSR@taylorandfrancis.com
Taylor & Francis Verlag GmbH, Kaufingerstraße 24, 80331 München, Germany

www.ingramcontent.com/pod-product-compliance
Lightning Source LLC
Chambersburg PA
CBHW061349300426
44116CB00011B/2049